The Closers 2
PART 2

The Sales Closer's Bible
Book Two

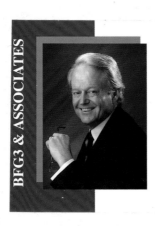

BFG3 & ASSOCIATES

BEN GAY III

Speaker
Sales Trainer • Consultant

Voice (800) 248-3555
(530) 622-7777
Fax (530) 295-9337
E-Mail: bfg3@directcon.net

P.O. Box 2481
Placerville, CA 95667-2481

BEN GAY III

The Closers 2 PART

© 1998 Ben Gay III

GAY III, Benjamin F.
    THE CLOSERS Part 2: Sales Closer's Bible

Library of Congress Catalog Card Number — 87-81170
ISBN 0-942645-08-1

Second Edition 1998
Printed in the United States of America
9 8 7 6 5 4 3 2 1

Editorial/Production — Hampton Books
Cover Design — C.M. Hyde
Cover Copy — C.M. Hyde
Typesetting — Sara Patton

Hampton Books
Box 67-8000 • Placerville, California 95667-8000
United States of America
Telephone: (530) 622-7777

Table of Contents

An Author's Beginning

I n 1979 I discovered a most unusual book. It was in very rough form and there were only 500 copies in existence. I bought them all, got the publishing and distribution rights, cleaned it up, promoted it, and turned it and its cassette program version into the all-time favorites of salespeople all over the world. Many call it *"that little blue book"*; others *"the sales closer's bible."* Most know it as simply *"The Closers."*

The Closers has been good to me and, as the rather unbelievable sales records show, I've been good for *The Closers.* More importantly, *The Closers* has been good for the countless salespeople all over the world who swear by it. If you don't have a copy of both *The Closers* book and *The Closers* cassette program, don't let the sun set on you again without obtaining your personal copies. And if you're a sales manager, make sure every single person you work with has *at least* the book in his or her briefcase! It has *literally* spelled the difference between success and failure for thousands upon thousands of top professional salespeople — The Master Closers of Selling.

For years, many of those same Master Closers have been after me to write another book on selling. And for years I have resisted — for a variety of reasons, not the least of which was laziness. But there were other reasons.

As you may know, writing can be agony. Why should I write *Son of The Closers,* since sales of *The Closers* itself continue to go up year after year? And why should I write another whole book on closing sales when no one I know has ever been able to fully put to use the material in *The Closers?* Myself included!

Here's what finally pushed me over the edge. An old friend of mine, one of the world's top sales pros, asked me why I thought it was fair to continue to hold back the real keys to becoming a Master Closer. At first I didn't understand his point. But, being a good friend, he continued to press me. I ducked and dodged my way through many phone conversations and several dinners before he finally nailed me with a sucker punch.

He asked me if I had given *The Closers* to my sons, both of whom are, at this writing, selling part-time while in school. I said, "Of course." Then he asked if that was all the help I had given them, and I heard myself saying, "Of course not! There's a whole lot more to selling than that! I'm teaching them how to be *sophisticated* salespeople. People who sell from strength. I'm teaching them the subtleties of selling. *The Closers* will just keep them afloat and give me time to teach them the real stuff — the important material. The material no one has ever put in a book."

It was too late! I'd said it out loud. I had spoken the awesome truth about *The Closers,* the most popular book and cassette program on selling and closing ever produced. It is wonderful as far as it goes. It will teach you how to close sales that others can't even dream of closing. It can turn you into a high-powered closing machine. It can make you the envy of all who see you perform. It can double your income — even triple or quadruple it! It can do things for your sales career that you can't imagine. But it can't turn you into a sophisticated, smooth, powerful, precision selling instrument. It wasn't designed to do that!

So, if you are ready to take the long but rewarding journey to professional selling at its highest levels, I am committed to giving you the same personal guidance I give my own clients, my own friends, and my own sons.

Where do we start? Well, first let me explain that learning how to be a top professional is not a matter of going from building block A to building block C to building block D, climaxing one glorious day at building block Z — at which point you have mastered the art of selling in its entirety. It doesn't work like that, because professional selling is an evolving, changing, living thing. You are changing. Acceptable forms of human behavior are changing. The language is changing. Yet, under all of that change, the basics haven't really changed that much. They just appear to have changed. _And you must too!_

Does that confuse you? It's supposed to. Because, until you turn loose of the old concept of "Teach me 25 closes and I'll go knock them dead," and/or "Give me the secret to selling in 25 buzzwords and let me at them," you are doomed to be an amateur for the rest of your sales career. Perhaps a highly paid amateur, but an amateur nevertheless.

No one wants to hear the truth about how the very best professional salespeople got there and stay there, but here it is. They have continued to learn. They pick up a piece here and there. They read books. They listen to tapes. They go to the seminars. They take notes. They try new ideas and discard old ones. They are constantly growing, learning, and evolving.

And they've come to understand that there is absolutely *no graduation day* for a true professional salesperson.

Further, they understand that the knowledge they need won't come in one blinding flash, nor in any one book or tape, nor at any one seminar, nor in one "magic close." Sales success doesn't come via UPS in one gift-wrapped package. Neither does any other important growth experience in life.

Ever try to learn to ride a bicycle? How about learning to become a parent? Or a husband or wife? Which book gave it to you? None, of course! So why would you expect the Laws of the Universe to be suspended just long enough for you to become a top professional salesperson? Obviously, they won't be. So, as with all other human endeavors, say "If it is to be, it's up to me." And then get on with the process!

I know that isn't the answer you want, nor was it the answer I wanted. It is, however, *the way it is!*

In *The Closers* we tell a nice little story to go along with the lessons. It makes the learning virtually painless — almost easy. But you have decided to go beyond that, so we'll remove the sugar coating and give you the information the way it comes to you in real life . . . at random, and when you are ready to absorb it.

Get yourself a highlighter pen and mark this book up. Wear it out. Dog-ear the pages. Paper clip the sections you need today, then move the paper clips to what you need tomorrow, then maybe back again. Remember, it is a never-ending process!

But when you just absolutely need a "fix" of specific easy closes, read *The Closers - Part 1* (the original version) again and listen to the tapes. Or call Hampton Books for their latest recommendations. *(They offer virtually every book and audio or video tape in the world, from virtually every publisher on earth!)* In the meantime, I'll share with you the information all major sales stars know and use every single selling day.

How It Began for Me

Although I was raised in a family of salespeople and used to love to hang out with the salespeople that worked for my father, I wasn't bright enough to understand that there was a skill involved in what they were doing. I just thought they were a bunch of charming folks who loved to chat with other people. So, in spite of a wonderful opportunity to learn, years went by without real benefit for me — except what I picked up totally by accident.

Then I went to work in a department store as a "salesperson" in the Housewares Department. Although I thought I was a salesperson at the time, I was only an order-taker. A semi-smart and aggressive order-taker, but an order-taker nonetheless.

I spent about five years with the store, won all sorts of contests, and left their organization having attended *one* short sales training session! *One!*

As little as was taught at that one session, I remember it as if it happened yesterday. They taught us to always have two or three items in front of the customer so we could say, "Which of these is best for you?" Then they taught us to always have a tie-in product for every item on the floor so we could say, "Let me show you a perfect addition to this!" And then, to get us over that awkward moment where we used to stand staring at the customer, they taught us to say, "Will that be cash or charge?"

That was it! That was the *entire* sales training program for one of the largest retail organizations in the world! But, primitive as it was, here's the punchline: *My sales doubled immediately!* And I was already one of their top *salespeople!* Scary, isn't it?

Well, I could barely spell salesperson, but I was hooked. And then it happened.

On September 14, 1965, I answered a business opportunity ad in *The Atlanta Journal.* I won't bore you with how unqualified I was to be looking at business opportunities.

Suffice it to say I was flat broke, poorly dressed, underweight, had remnants of my high school acne, and sported a flat-top. At 23, I was a pitiful sight to say the least!

The man who ran the ad was named Bill Dempsey. I didn't know it at the time, but he was a Master Closer in every aspect of the word. He would come to be a good friend and is an influence in my life to this day. Trust me when I tell you that I never had a chance!

Now understand this: Much of what I'm going to tell you about Bill Dempsey, and many of the other Superstars of Selling who I've known over the years, is based on hind-sight —*especially* in those early years. When I say he (or they) "closed someone," understand I didn't know the meaning of the word "close" at the time. I had never heard *anything* about sales training. I didn't know beans about *any* aspect of selling. My only contribution to the process in the first year or two was lots of energy, a desire to learn, and a need for money to support me and my bride.

O.K., *from hindsight:* Dempsey qualified me like no one has ever been qualified before — except for probably everyone else he had ever worked with! In what I thought was a casual conversation, I told him things I doubt I had ever told anyone before. He knew about my background, my family, my friends, my social life, my job, my income, my goals (what few there were), my hopes, my dreams, my fears, the car I drove, and my checkbook balance — *everything!*

And then, with my miserable situation clearly laid out in front of us, he showed me how to get from where I was to where, in my *wildest* dreams, I really wanted to be. As you might have guessed, it turned out that the solution to ALL of my problems was to join his organization!

But it gets better!

Although I literally didn't have enough money to get my

car out of the office building's parking garage, and although my wife and I were living hand to mouth, he sold me on a package that totaled a little over $5,000 *(in 1965 dollars!)*. Over $5,000, when I didn't have 50 spare cents to my name!

Now I said he "sold me," but it didn't end there. As you know, selling a high-ticket item to an unqualified prospect is a joke. He'll *buy* all right, but he *won't pay* — because he *can't!*

I guess old Dempsey knew the sale would come unstuck if it was *his* sale, so he just sped up the process. *He* unstuck it! He took it back! He told me that, as much as he liked me, I didn't have a chance of raising the $5,000 needed. And I had no sales experience, so I'd probably fail anyway — and he wasn't going to take that responsibility on himself.

He rose from his chair, extended his hand, and wished me the best. I couldn't believe what was happening! The opportunity of a lifetime was before me and this man was telling me I couldn't participate. *No way!*

Time and space doesn't allow a complete rendition of my sales presentation to Dempsey, but trust me when I tell you it was *magnificent!* It must have been because, when I was finished, he *reluctantly* agreed to accept my $5,000 — if I could raise it all within a week. *No problem!*

Understand that my raising $5,000 within a week of September 14, 1965 was like you flying to Mars on top of your child's kite. There wasn't a chance of it happening . . . so you'll understand my feeling of pride when I handed him a cashier's check for $5,000 just seven days later!

That was my entry into big-time, powerhouse selling. I remember leaving his office with a strange feeling. I had witnessed something I didn't even know existed. A stranger had been able to analyze me, take me apart mentally, reassemble me in a different form, redirect my thinking, gently force me to a decision, relieve me of a large sum of money . . .

and make me feel good about it. All in about an hour. All with mere words, the sheer force of his personality, and a learned skill — a skill I was determined to learn!

Dempsey was a power closer, but not "high pressure." Only amateurs have to resort to anything a customer can see, sense, and dislike. By power closing, I mean I was swept up in the logic of his presentation. In the depth of his obvious belief. In his integrity. In his gentle take-it-or-leave-it attitude. He had the courage to walk up to the very edge of a sale and almost dare you not to buy. His confidence was extremely evident. You could feel it! In a positive way, I was almost afraid of him — as one might be with a strong father figure. I was actually relieved when he allowed me to buy — the pressure I had put on myself left me and I was very satisfied with my decision. I had met a force I didn't understand — but I was determined to know what he knew!

A New World Opens for Me

So I don't leave you hanging, everything that Bill Dempsey told me would happen, DID. I made more money the first twelve months I was in the business than I would have made in the next ten years the way I had been going. I was able to travel all over the country, then all over the world. Private jets, yachts, and chauffeur-driven cars became a normal part of my life. Tailor-made suits became as natural as torn jeans had been. I met with, worked with, and became friends with many of the rich and powerful. Because of Bill Dempsey's sales closing skills, my life changed . . . and nothing has been the same since!

That said, let me tell you that all of the money, glamour, and excitement were the least of it — although I didn't realize it at the time.

Far more important than the money, I had fallen into an environment that may not have existed before . . . and may never again. The company I had joined was a multi-level direct sales cosmetic company called Holiday Magic. In its day, it was one of the largest companies of its kind in the world. And it began at about the same time formalized modern sales and motivational training began to catch fire. Therefore, if only by accident, virtually everyone who was anyone in sales and/or sales training was involved with the company — either as an actual distributor or as part of the companies we hired to motivate and train our people.

I won't try to put everything and everyone in chronological order, but suffice it to say that if you were important in direct sales during that period of time, you probably worked with or for the company, or for one of its many support organizations. It was a magical time for a young man like me . . . and, because the company was young and growing rapidly, I rose through the ranks quicker than I had any reason to expect. I held six different positions in a little over two years, and became president of the entire organization at about the age most of my friends were trying to figure out what they should do after college.

I don't tell you this to brag, only to explain why a young, inexperienced kid was able to become involved with the legends of sales and sales training. Sure, I worked hard. And I studied even harder. But a *great deal* of what I've experienced over the past three decades has been, at its root, due to sheer luck. I answered the right ad on the right day. I was interviewed by the right man (*I thank God he was a power closer!*). And just as I stepped on board, the whole company took off like a rocket and I was in for the ride of my life!

The Cast of Characters

First, to those sales greats whose names are left out of this book, let me apologize. Time dulls the memory, and too many names and personal stories would tend to clutter the concept. But, whether you are mentioned or not, know that what you shared with me and all of the others was and is *deeply* appreciated.

Now set the scene in your mind. One of our distributors was then a little-known raw talent by the name of **Zig Ziglar.** And his partner was a *real* power closer named **Mel Lanius. Bill Dempsey** was there, of course. And just down the road in Cedartown, Georgia was a man who was paid to train us — the legendary **Fred Herman** of *Keep It Simple, Salesmen* fame.

Then the company hired the major force in sales training of that era, **American Salesmasters** of Denver, Colorado. In that package of talent came some of the all-time heavyweight salespeople and sales trainers who ever lived: **Hal Krause, Bob Albin, Cavett Robert, Bob Richards, J. Douglas Edwards,** and *many, many* others!

Later we hired the **Wilson Learning Corporation** of Minneapolis, Minnesota to also aid in our sales training. In that package of talent we learned what was then called Sales Sonics from **Larry Wilson, Bill Gove,** and an *entire team* of true top sales professionals. The very best in the world at the time!

And somewhere along the line, we retained **Earl Nightingale** to be the voice of Holiday Magic. Through this association, we began rubbing elbows with just about everyone else who had ever excelled in the modern sales world.

But it wasn't all from the outside. In addition to the sales pros who had been drawn to the company to begin with, this fantastic atmosphere began creating and generating its own sales legends: **Jim Hearn, Larry Proffit,** the great **Walter Wells,** and hundreds of others over the years. And it generated the best power closer I've ever seen work in almost 30 years of selling, **James H. Rucker, Jr.** He was *absolutely unbelievable!*

Now keep in mind, I wasn't watching these people on a videotape, or listening to them in my car, or sitting in the balcony of an auditorium watching them through binoculars. I was sitting in actual sales presentations with them. I held seminars with them. Traveled with them. Dined with them. They visited my home and I visited theirs. Many worked _for_ me, all worked _with_ me.

As I said earlier, I don't believe an environment like that had ever existed before. I can assure you it will never exist again, because audio and video cassette programs are now a much more efficient way to deliver training. Efficient, YES — but the hands-on magic is _gone forever!_

As I also said earlier, learning how to be a real sales professional doesn't come in a neat package from UPS. Mine didn't and yours won't. It _must_ come in bits and pieces — as it occurs to the teacher, and as the student is ready to accept it. And it must be taught different ways at different times and with different words — although the actual number of sales _secrets_ actually numbers less than twenty, grand total!

So why not just list the "secrets" and be done with it? Because they aren't simple to explain nor to learn. If they were, all salespeople would now be sales professionals as a result of attending one brief sales training seminar on a Saturday afternoon — and all sales trainers would be out of work.

But here's some good news for you: I was and am an excellent notetaker. Over the years I have written down and/or recorded just about everything of importance I've seen or heard. And my notes on selling are among the largest category in my personal library. To the extent that time and space will allow, I'm going to share that information with you in this book _(The Closers 2),_ and I'll keep going until I'm out of notes and proven ideas. Maybe we'll all live to see _The Closers Part 32!_ So rest assured, there's **more to come!**

Watch Out!

No one's sales education should begin or end with *The Closers Part 2*. I encourage you to attend lots of seminars. Read many books. Listen to the audio tapes and watch the videotapes. Even in the worst of them, you'll find nuggets of sales gold — but you *must* filter out the nonsense or it will ruin you! There are *many false prophets* in the sales training world!

At the risk of sounding like an old man talking about the good old days, or saying "When I was growing up . . . ," let me tell you there has been a real change in the quality of sales trainers over the last twenty years. Most of that change has *not* been for the better!

Here's how Fred Herman got started as a sales trainer, for instance. FIRST he was a top salesman. THEN his boss asked him to tell the others how he was doing it. *Doing it* being the important part of that sentence! And that's how most of the other sales trainers of that era, myself included, got started. We were simply telling other salespeople on Saturday how we were doing it out in the field during the week. In other words, FIRST we were successful salespeople in our own right.

Today there are only a few sales trainers around who actually had a successful selling career of their own. There are even fewer who are still actually involved in selling anything on a day-to-day basis!

The vast majority of today's sales training *"experts"* fall into one of two categories:

1. People who've never sold anything successfully in their lives — except for their own speeches, books, tapes, and seminars on what you should do. They've found it's easier to stand at the front of a room and tell you what to do than it is to go out and do it themselves — *much easier!*

2. People who did have at least a semi-successful sales career, but it ended thirty years ago! They, therefore, are forced

to teach how it *used to be* — as best they can remember it, plus what they've heard might work.

As the title of this section says, "Watch out!" Be careful where you get your sales training input!

Here We Go!

I'm now going to begin sharing from my own personal files, notes, and memory. And, although I've learned these lessons over a long period of time and from many different sources, for ease of writing and because of my personal regard for him, I'm going to attribute the lessons learned mainly to one source. He was the strongest salesperson and power closer I've ever seen. His name? James H. Rucker, Jr.

Fortunately, I took really good notes during the years I worked with him, because Jimmy, as he preferred to be called, was a *natural* salesperson. By that I mean, he never had any formal sales training to speak of, and couldn't begin to tell you how he made sales presentations and closed sales. *He just did!* And he used to wonder why we all didn't do the same.

When we'd ask him how he did it, he'd just say, "I just talk to people and share the opportunity to buy." Trust me, there was a whole lot more to Rucker than that!

Well, here's what Jimmy (and all the others) tried to teach me. Perhaps you can benefit from their wisdom too.

Ben Gay III

The First Step
to Sales Success

So you've memorized twenty-three tricky closes. You can now come back with fifty-one objection retorts. You know what customers are going to say before they do. You are honed to a *razor's edge.* You're like a steel trap waiting for your next customer to step into your sales closing grasp.

And in spite of all of this, you still feel a little less than adequate. You still aren't the top salesperson in your company or, certainly, in your industry. You still aren't a Master Closer.

What's wrong?

Well, without knowing you personally, it's difficult to say with absolute accuracy. But I've been selling, teaching, and consulting in the sales industry for almost thirty years, so I *can* tell you what those symptoms mean in the majority of cases. And I can tell you how to cure that slightly sickening queasy feeling you often have. The feeling you've never even told your wife or husband about. The feeling that makes you wonder if selling is an honorable profession — or if it can even be practiced by honorable people.

Here's the first step to being a first-class, happy, successful, and honorable Master Closer: Give serious consideration to quitting your job today. Yes, that's what I said! And actually resign right away if you aren't totally convinced you are selling a product or service that you are personally wild about. A product that makes you feel the joy of sharing something of value every time you make a sale. A product that you would personally purchase at an even higher price if you weren't already selling it. A product you would enthusiastically sell at full price to your mother. To your father. To your best friend.

I'm deadly serious. If your current sales position doesn't come up to that high standard, get out!

The world is full of products and services that will pass this personal test. And, until you are *enthusiastically* selling one of them, you aren't living up to your potential — personally or financially. In fact, until you are selling something you can feel this way about, you are little more than a well-dressed, sophisticated, carnival barker.

The great sales trainer J. Douglas Edwards and I were chatting on the phone many years ago. He said something I'll never forget. He said that, after years of study, he had come to the conclusion that there was only one significant difference between a good con man and an honorable Master Closer. And that difference was simply belief in a good quality product. You see, the techniques of helping a person make a decision are almost identical. But the con man is in it only for the money, while the honorable Master Closer believes strongly and rightfully in the value of his or her product.

And the honorable Master Closer always remembers the lesson taught in *The Closers. Sum Tertius — I Am Third.*

Sell the Benefits!

Did you know that only about one out of a hundred people who claim to have read *Think and Grow Rich* actually has? Did you know that only about one out of a thousand people who claim to have read the Bible actually has? Did you know that virtually all salespeople who have been in selling over 24 hours claim to "sell the benefits, not the features," but that less than one in two thousand actually does?

Why is that?

Well, there are only two major reasons: One is that the salespeople in question are mentally lazy; tend to give poor, unprofessional sales presentations; and generally tend to be part of the 80% of salespeople who only make 20% of the total sales.

The second reason is easier to deal with, it being that the average salesperson still doesn't really know the difference between a feature and a benefit. And *that's curable!*

Whether you and/or the people working with you need some work in this area, here's an interesting drill you can use.

Although it sounds like Basic Salesmanship 101, you need to list *all* of the features of your product down the left side of a sheet of paper. ALL of them! Then and only then, you should list the corresponding *benefit to the customer* that each feature helps deliver.

For example, don't try to sell me your widget because it has a heavy duty stainless steel handle. I don't care. Instead, tell me how securely that handle keeps the widget door in place, protecting all of the things I tend to store in my widget. And tell me how I'll never have to replace, polish, or otherwise think about maintaining that handle ever again. The actual handle is a mere feature. What it *does for me* is a benefit.

Don't take me on a tour of the property and tell me there is a 55-acre lake. So what? Tell me how much I'll enjoy swimming in it as a property owner/member. Help me picture my grandchildren fishing on its banks. The lake is a feature. What I get to do on it, in it, and around it are benefits. Don't tell me you've got a lake. I couldn't care less. What's in it for *me?!*

The nose on your face is a feature. Getting to breathe through it is a benefit.

A 300-horsepower engine is a feature. Getting to highway speed quickly and safely is a benefit.

Your customers think your product's features are nice. Even mildly interesting. But what they are all silently yelling at you is *What's in it for me?! What's in it for me?!* **What's in it for me?!"**

And you don't even have to be subtle about it. Until you get good at doing it naturally and smoothly, try these phrases:

"*Ms. Prospect, here's an interesting feature — but let me explain the direct benefit to you . . .*"

"*Mr. Prospect, a lot of people first notice this doo-dad — but let me show you what it does for YOU . . .*"

"*Mr. and Mrs. Prospect, I'll cover some of the unique features of this product for you — but, if you're like me and my husband [or wife], what you REALLY want to know is, 'What's in it for us?' So let me show you the direct benefits you'll enjoy by owning this wonderful gartensplot!*"

See? No one really cares about your roll bar. They care about THEIR head. They don't want your 3hp drill. They want THEIR ¼-inch holes! They don't want your aerodynamically designed boat. They want to have fun with THEIR family and impress THEIR friends! They want to feel the wind in THEIR hair! They want to be *young* again!

So first discover what the benefits are. Then memorize them — almost to the exclusion of the features. Then make them part of the way you naturally talk.

*Sell the benefits! Sell the benefits! **Sell the benefits!***

Sales Pros Are
Always Changing

Years ago the late Hubert Humphrey endeared himself to me and many others when he appeared on *Meet the Press* or one of the television interview programs of the day. It was during the 1968 Presidential campaign and a reporter was pressing him hard on some subject, gleefully pointing out that Humphrey's current position on some policy question was in direct and complete opposition to his stated and well-known position on the same issue back in 1945.

I remember thinking that the reporter really had him trapped, but then Mr. Humphrey taught me a lesson I've never forgotten. He said something to the effect that he was proud of the fact that not just *that* position had changed over the 23 years that had passed, but that *many* of his opinions and beliefs had changed in that period of time. And he went on to explain that some of his current positions would surely change and evolve as he became older and wiser, and as more information became available to him. He stated that he was running for President as a seasoned 57-year-old professional, and that surely the voters wouldn't want him clinging doggedly to the positions he had held as an inexperienced 34-year-old novice public servant.

I was only 26 years old when I heard Mr. Humphrey and his explanation of the benefits of personal growth and evolvement, but it made a permanent change in my attitude and approach to life and to professional selling.

Although it may be a little unsettling to think that almost all of our current beliefs — other than the basics of honesty, loyalty, etc. — are going to change in the years ahead (some slightly, some completely), the alternative is far worse.

Imagine reaching age 65, a time by which we should certainly have achieved at least some growth and gained some experience, only to discover we are still intellectually the same person we were at 20. It is a frightening thought for anyone who remembers what he or she believed at 20, I assure you!

We are constantly evolving. Therefore, we must constantly let go. It's O.K. to say "I was wrong," or "But look at what I've learned since then." There should be no pride in defending old, worn-out, outdated, and incorrect conclusions and techniques. We are supposed to get better as we get older! And better, *by definition,* means what we fear so much: *change.*

Here's an example of "letting go" that I really treasure. Robert Browning, the British poet, was holding court for the London Poetry Society back in the late 1800s when the members asked him for an interpretation of an unusually obscure passage of his poetry. Brown read it, read it again, and then read it again. Finally, he shrugged his shoulders and sighed, "When I wrote that, God and I knew what it meant, but now God alone knows."

If Hubert Humphrey and Robert Browning both learned the value of "letting go" of old, worn-out ideas, perhaps you and I should work on it too.

Qualify But
Don't Prejudge!

Seems like not a day goes by that at least one salesperson tells us another horror story about prejudging a prospect. The story almost always ends with the amount of commission dollars lost as a result of this terrible mistake.

And then we get letters saying, "But you tell us to prequalify our prospects!" Both positions are, of course, true, because they are two entirely different subjects.

To qualify a prospect is to talk with him/her about needs, wants, timeframes, financial position, etc., *before* launching into your terribly effective, totally canned presentation #147. The reason being that this particular customer may need to hear your terribly effective, totally canned presentation #29 instead.

Or, just perhaps, a highly personalized presentation built around his/her own desires, needs, and wants — a presentation you may have never given in your entire sales life.

That, in a very small nutshell, is qualifying or prequalifying. Prejudging someone is, on the other hand, totally different and totally wrong about 89% of the time!

My first bad experience — and I've had many — came when I was a young salesman in a combination camera and sporting goods department in a large store. I was alone in the department when two customers entered from opposite ends of the area. One, a very well-dressed gentleman, walked into the sporting goods section. The other man, older and fatter, and dressed in dirty overalls, walked into the camera department. My lightning-quick computerlike mind sized up the situation instantly. I circled around a display to avoid eye contact with the obviously broke dirt farmer and zeroed in on "Mr. Success."

Since you already know the basic ending, I'll make the story shorter: My "obviously" highly qualified customer proceeded to tie up almost an hour of my time and wound up spending less than $25 on the cheapest pair of cardboard shoulder pads and helmet we carried. They were for his 5-year-old son. Then, to add insult to injury, when I called upstairs for an authorization, the Credit Department told me to seize his credit card!

Meanwhile, over at the camera counter, my hayseed friend had managed to catch the eye of my fellow salesman, who was just returning from lunch. The sale went like wildfire! The customer knew exactly what he wanted. He needed no advice. He just pointed to things. And when his buying fury ended, he pulled out over $2,500 in rumpled old bills (CASH!), paid for everything, and walked out of the department. And friends, that was $2,500 in 1960 dollars!

How would I have handled the situation today? Well, first I would have approached *both* gentlemen and explained my predicament. Then I would have asked if either was in a huge rush, and if either already knew exactly what he wanted. This would have allowed me to service both men politely. It would have also kept both men as my customers, even if my friend had returned from lunch when he did. And, most probably, I would have first been with the camera customer . . . then with "Mr. Success."

See, my error had nothing to do with qualifying my customers. I never got that far! My mistake was in **prejudging** the gentlemen and, as a result, I was 100% wrong with *both* men.

Want to hear a cute story? What reminded me to do a segment on this subject was a call I got from my oldest son last night. He is away at college, but works part-time in a jewelry store. Seems he was sitting behind the counter doing a complimentary watch cleaning and installing a $6.50 watch battery which he had "sold." In walked an overweight, poorly dressed lady who appeared, at first glance, to be extremely rushed and in a very bad mood. Using the lightning-quick computerlike mind he inherited from God-only-knows-where, he sized up the situation instantly. He avoided eye contact with the lady and signaled one of his associates in the back room. The sales associate walked out and the lady said . . . well, you *know* what she said!

Seems she had been looking at a particular ring for about a month. She pointed at it, pulled out her credit card (which cleared with no problem), slipped it onto her finger, and was gone in less than 5 minutes! And it cost about the same as what my great camera sale totaled!

My son asked, "Dad, when do you learn not to do that?" I said, "I don't know, son. I just don't know."

Qualify **everyone**! Don't prejudge **anyone**!

★ ★ ★

Prepare Your
Sales Skills Now!

Few things beat preparation, whether in our personal or selling lives. President Truman said, "What a man does on some great occasion will be determined by what he already is. And what he is will be determined by years of prior preparation. So, if a man does not prepare himself, when his great opportunity comes, it will only make him appear foolish."

That's pretty strong stuff, but then, Harry Truman was made of strong stuff. And, of course, he was living proof of what he said, as he showed the world clearly in early 1945.

Vice President Truman may have been an unknown quantity to casual or uninformed observers when President Roosevelt died suddenly at Warm Springs, Georgia, but those who knew Truman were aware that he had spent the previous 61 years preparing for his great opportunity — whatever it was to be.

The librarian in Independence, Missouri, said that Truman had read virtually every book in the library by the time he was in his early teens. Now *that's* preparation if I ever heard of it!

So how does this apply to those of us in selling? Well, we never know when our great opportunity will come . . . or how many great opportunities we'll be offered, but we should know that *preparation* will be the key to how we handle them.

Gene Fowler, the novelist, gave a humorous but true example of how lack of preparation can truly make you appear foolish. It seems that as a shy young boy, Gene had his eyes set on a lovely girl in his school class. Assuming she would have no interest in him, he didn't do his homework, his *preparation.* Then, at a high school dance, and with absolutely no warning, his great opportunity came. The girl made a strong and unmistakable play for him. She flattered him. She gently teased him. She looked longingly into his eyes and then she said, "A penny for your thoughts," to which Gene Fowler replied, "I was just wondering whether a horse's legs ever go to sleep on him."

What will come spilling out of your mouth when your once-in-a-lifetime selling situation presents itself? Will you be ready to take full advantage of it? You will if you prepare NOW! Read the books. Listen to and watch the tapes. Go to the seminars. Like you tell your customers, pay the price!

I Don't Know!

You have just read three of the most difficult words to pronounce in the English language and probably in any other language!

Although just about everyone suffers from the inability to say those three simple words, salespeople find them *especially* troublesome. As a result, thousands of sales are lost every single day.

Here's a concept that all top sales professionals and all Master Closers finally had to understand before they really hit their maximum potential and stride. It is very simple to explain, but very difficult to practice while out on the firing line in the heat of battle. It is this:

There are basically three ways to answer any question:

1. You have an honest and positive answer (i.e., Yes, we can do that.").

2. You have an honest and negative answer (i.e., No, we can't do that.")

3. You have an honest answer that is neither positive or negative (i.e., "I honestly don't know the answer to that question.").

Why do you suppose salespeople have such difficulty with that third option? Do they think guessing is better? That lying is more effective? That they'd look stupid if they didn't have an immediate answer to every conceivable question ever put to them? What is it about salespeople that makes this simple concept so difficult?

Well, whatever it is, here are a few solid reasons for using **"I don't know,"** softened by, "but I'll find out, if it is important to you."

First, it is the honest way to handle a question when you don't know, and that should be enough.

Second, it shows your customer that you are honest and not just trying to dazzle him with footwork.

Third, it gives you extra time to think. Therefore, when you do give your honest answer, it can be more effectively phrased.

Fourth, it will help you avoid traps set by customers. Did you know that surveys show many of the questions you are asked during your sales presentations are not questions at all? They are tests of your integrity and product knowledge! The customer knew the correct answer before he asked you!

Fifth, it helps maintain your credibility as an expert in your field. Understand that experts frequently have to look up information before they respond to questions. Albert Einstein didn't even know how many feet there were in a mile! He said that's why he had all those books. Do you think less of him for not knowing? Of course not! But there's nothing worse than having a "guesstimate" explode in your face just as you are trying to close a sale.

Sixth, it shows you really care about your customers. It takes a person who cares to make sure his/her customers get the straight scoop — even if it takes a little longer.

Remember the old story of the boss yelling at his people, "I want it Thursday"? And one brave soul in his organization mustered his courage and said, "Do you want it _right,_ or do you want it on Thursday? We can't do both." Supposedly, he was promoted on the spot! If not, he should have been.

Your customers are the same way. They'd certainly prefer the answer now, but they want it right when they do get it.

Go ahead and try it! Say, **"I don't know, but I'll find out."** Not so hard, is it? Next time try it in front of a customer!

So, how many feet are there in a mile? I really don't know, but I'll find out, if it's really important to you. Write to me.

Cash In On
SNAFU's

You must know your competition as well as you know your own products/services. This constant emphasis is usually designed to prepare you for selling against a competitor's lower prices, different quality, faster shipping, customer service, etc. SNAFU selling (from the paraphrased World War II saying, "Situation normal, all fouled up") is a side benefit of that knowledge — a bonus, if you will.

In order to learn as much about your competitor's products/services as you know about your own, you're obviously going to have to generate a great deal of inside information about them. This means you'll have to know not only what you are up against, but *who* you are up against and how they are performing.

One top salesperson we know studies not only his competition at the local level, he owns one share of stock in every publicly held competitor he sells against. This one share puts him on the stockholders' list, giving him direct access to a blizzard of information about his rivals — material his customers would probably never see *(without his help)*.

Now, in addition to straight competitive day-to-day selling, he has additional ammunition others don't have. This gives him opportunities to go after weak spots in his competitor's soft underbelly. Whether it is a local, regional, national, or international problem the competition is having, you can rest assured his customers will hear about it at the appropriate moment.

Understand, he isn't selling negatively or knocking his competition. He operates as a third-party counselor when he sells. An expert. A source of industry information. In fact, he also frequently shares good information about his competition with his customers!

He says he finds the extra tool of inside information especially effective in cracking open new accounts he hasn't been able to get to before. And in expanding business with customers who have been giving him only token business in the past. And, of course, in maintaining those customers who already regard him as an expert in his field — because his advanced, in-depth knowledge of current and future events simply confirms his position as an authority.

During a particular sales presentation, his customer was beating him about the head and shoulders because of his product's pricing. The customer ranted and raved that the XYZ Company listed virtually the same product at a price 17% lower than his. His response? He said, "Well, frankly speaking, that price is totally irrelevant!" That gave our friend the opening he needed to point out that the competitor had just lost a major supplier of their raw material, and faced a long and bitter strike at their manufacturing plant. The point being, they weren't going to be able to supply the product at *any* price! The 17% price differential was, therefore, meaningless.

How did he know this? His stockbroker had given him a "sell" recommendation for the one share of stock he held . . . and the recommendation came with a complete explanation as to why he should sell!

How's that for having a leg up on the competition? That's SNAFU selling at its best! And do you want to know the punchline? Not only did he get the business at the higher price, he has kept it — because the competitor's salesman wasn't able to share this important inside information about his own company for another three weeks. Why? He simply didn't know about it!

Watch for SNAFU's, then spring into action while the wound is still fresh and bleeding.

Don't Let 'Em Distract You

Things aren't always what they seem, are they? That's a lesson we've all learned time and time again. But the problem seems to be that we learn the lesson each time after it has happened to us again. The trick, if there is one, might be to investigate our assumptions first — before we make the error that leads us to our crystal-clear 20/20 hindsight, especially in sales!

We see it every single day. People accept a given premise without question, then build a whole series of actions on what turns out to be an incorrect starting point.

Magicians do it to us deliberately, and it is fun and harmless. They'll tell us that the hat is empty — which it isn't. Or that there is nothing up their sleeve — when their sleeve is full of things. They'll gesture dramatically in one direction to get our attention — when the important movement is in exactly the opposite direction. Well, in a magic show it is simply good entertainment. But in real life, with real situations, with real customers, that same mental blind spot can lead to disaster.

When I joined the Coast Guard many years ago, I was taught to check my references. To never assume *anything*. The knot that appeared to be securely tied might not be. At sea, you'd be surprised how much north, south, east, and west look alike, especially in a storm or at night, when we needed the information most. And an unchecked life jacket or life raft might sink like a stone if you assumed it was in good repair.

Once, early in my business career, I was faced with unraveling a mystery as to who was telling me the truth in a case of possible fraud involving several thousands of dollars. I was hearing new stories and new excuses on an hourly basis. I was bewildered by the web of confusion surrounding the total transaction. There were about a dozen players involved, and each had a story absolving himself and another story implicating one or more of the others.

Finally I went to my boss, one of my early mentors, with the problem. I got out a legal pad and began drawing circles, arrows, and dollar signs. Then, as I began to relate one of the many versions I'd heard, he stopped me and said, "Ben, they've distracted you. Who got the money?" When I told him, he threw my notes in the trash can and reminded me that rarely did a group of guilty people conspire to steal money and give it to an innocent person.

There it was again! **Check your references. Don't be distracted! Assume nothing!**

This doesn't mean you can't trust anyone. It just means that, in matters of importance *(selling, for example)*, you should check your references. When a magician holds up a rabbit, says it is alive, and stuffs it in a trick cannon, it isn't really important whether he is telling you the truth or not. But when a *business* magician tells you the property will never flood — **check your references!** Or when a person hands you a parachute and tells you it is O.K. to jump — **check the chute!** In fact, a whole business training film was made on that one point, called "Pack Your Own Chute."

Or, as the old gamblers will tell you, "Trust everyone. Then cut the cards."

Here's a cute but true story to help you remember the lesson: A friend of Vernon Duke, the famous composer, accosted him on the street one day, complaining bitterly about the weather he had encountered in Paris during a recent two-week visit. Duke listened patiently, then asked, "But why are you mad at me?"

"Because," his friend said, "I went there based on your song, *April in Paris,* and the weather was terrible in April!"

Duke chuckled, then apologized and explained, "I thought everyone knew that the weather in Paris was terrible during April. I really meant May, but the rhythm of the song required a two-syllable month!"

You see, you've just got to check your references! Don't be distracted. And don't assume anything! Especially when a customer/prospect is giving you objections. Or pleading poverty. Or stalling. Or ducking and weaving. Or waving his imitation Rolex watch in your face. *Check your references!*

Selling Points
Checklist

We were reviewing a new direct mail piece this morning, making sure we hit all of the selling points on our standard checklist. Although many are specific to direct mail only, some are important and applicable to all sales efforts. Let me share a few of them, encouraging you to Technicolor and flesh out your sales presentations with them.

1. **Be specific** in explaining the benefits of your product or service. Don't just say your product is a timesaver, if you can back that up with a statement such as, "Studies have shown that our typical customer saves 31 minutes a day with this, and that's over 188 hours a year, or about 5 full weeks of man-hours!"

2. Back up specifics with **written testimonials** whenever possible. You saying your product/service is wonderful is interesting, but other customers saying it is *sales closing power!*

3. You've given specific examples of benefits. You've backed them up with written testimonials. Now **guarantee what you've promised**, both orally and in writing.

4. When you are selling against direct competition, **know their product/service** as well as you know your own. Then, from a position of knowledge and strength, show and invite comparisons. Note: If your product/service isn't the best even after you've added your own secret ingredient to the offer (you!), or if your product/service just won't stand up to the bright white light of comparison — then you're selling the wrong item!

5. If your product/service lends itself to it, **use trial offers**. If you and what you are selling are strong enough, a no-risk trial period is a powerful convincer. Similar to what J. Douglas Edwards called the Puppy Dog Close, letting your customer actually use and benefit from your widget is hard to beat. And if it really works like you said it would, you'll have a hard time getting it back after the trial period!

Understand, these five selling tips are NOT designed to replace your sales presentation. Just make sure they are in it. Let them serve as enhancers — like Hamburger Helper!

Do You Own One?

Although he certainly wasn't the first to use it, my father had an effective way of selling real estate in a tiny little development in Southern California. It was in the late 1940s and his job was to put together a sales team to sell property in a place that looked like where Apollo 11 set down on the moon. It was, to say the least, bleak land!

The first thing he did was to purchase a home there — one of the very first. The second thing he did was to make it a requirement that all of the salespeople he employed owned at least a building lot and that they paid the normal full price for it. In fact, that was his first real qualifier. If you didn't believe in his dream enough to live there, he didn't want you selling others on the idea.

Then he developed a set route and a word-for-word script for a tour of the entire development. This enabled the sales-people to all tell the same truthful and effective story about the planned community. The only allowed deviation from the master script being when you took a "detour" and went past your *own* home or building lot. Dad said it was by far the most powerful part of the sales presentation — a fact backed up by the sales results!

Although I was only about 6 years old when we first moved there, that part of the sales presentation stayed with me for years. Then, as a young married man, I took my wife and first son down to visit the area. The salesman we met at the hotel took us on tour and gave us basically the same scripted tour my father had written so many years before, even right down to a "detour" by his own house!

The scripted tour must have worked. I just got off the phone with the mayor of the little town that was nothing but barren high desert country in the 1940s. The mayor told me that there are now 58,740 people living there, including the King of the Cowboys, Roy Rogers, and his wife, Dale Evans! The town? Apple Valley, California.

Enough nostalgia. Back to the real subject: Do you own one? You see, if you don't own one, it makes me wonder if you really believe.

Whether it's a building lot at Apple Valley or a week of your own at a timeshare resort, I want to know if you are in with me. Don't try to sell me a Cadillac while your Honda is hidden around behind the dealership. And don't suck my pillows flat demonstrating your Rainbow vacuum cleaner while your wife uses her Hoover upright at home. Because if I see that, I just won't do business with you.

It has been said that "What you are speaks so loudly, I can't hear a word you're saying." And that's doubly true in selling!

What if you sell oil tankers? That's just the exception that proves the rule! For the rest of us, be your own first customer!

When You're Hit With a "Two by Four"

My style of selling and of sales training is based on preparation, training, practice, and "the set-up." All my years out in the sales trenches have convinced me that absolutely nothing beats that devastating combination.

Why? Because most of selling is *totally* predictable! Let's be honest, how many different ways can you present your super-duper widget? And, realistically, how many different questions or objections can they have to it?

Oh sure, there is always the unusual "new question" — but you and I know it's very rare and that it's usually based on something unique to them and them alone. Like my friend who was demonstrating unicycles in a sporting goods store. He did a full presentation and promised the audience that all buyers would learn how to ride their unicycles before they left the store that afternoon — no matter how awkward or clumsy they might be. Just then a man in the back row raised his hand and said he'd buy one if it really had that guarantee. My friend said, "It sure does! Come on up! We'll give you your lesson right now!"

The crowd parted to make way for him and there he stood — supported by a crutch and one leg.

Now I promise you, as thorough as the Unicycle Sales Training Seminar probably was, it didn't cover this one-of-a-kind situation (although it probably does now!).

No training, no preparation, no practice, and no set-up can possibly cover every single conceivable selling situation that will ever happen to you. But, since all that prior work will cover about 97% of your selling opportunities, let me encourage you to *prepare, train, practice,* and do your *set-up* constantly.

O.K., let's deal with the other 3%, where you'll encounter your own personal one-legged unicycle prospects.

You are giving or have given your best sales presentation. Everything is sailing along beautifully, the cash register bell is ringing in your head, your order book is calling out to you, the time is here — then, BANG! He hits you with it! The one you've never heard. The one you weren't ready for. The one for which you have no snappy rejoinder. Now what do you do?

Learn the following five-step solution, complete with a sixth step escape hatch for emergencies, and you'll save 90% of those situations — assuming, of course, you are selling a worthwhile product at a reasonable price to a qualified prospect.

First, resist the temptation to instantly fill the air with "sales babble." Don't let the silence panic you. Gather your thoughts. It's entirely possible that, given a few seconds, you

DO have the proper response buried somewhere deep within you. Give it time to rise to the surface. Concentrate on looking thoughtful — not stunned. Your prospect would rather have a correct answer in thirty seconds than an instant incorrect answer, I assure you! And here's a bonus I've found using this technique. Frequently my customers have become so unnerved by my silence that they said something to the effect of, "Oh, never mind. That wasn't important anyway."

Second, if you aren't lucky enough to be bailed out by your customer and do have to come up with an answer (now or later), preface your response with, "That's a really good question! I don't think I've ever been asked that before." That will make your customer feel important, intelligent, and indebted to you. It sets him up to receive your answer in a positive light or, if you simply don't have an answer at the moment, it explains why. His question was so good you couldn't be expected to have an instant solution! And you care enough about him to not just make something up. In other words, he is *brilliant* and you are *honest* and *concerned* — a wonderful combination!

Third, have him work with you — just to make sure you really understand what his concern really is. Start by repeating his objection back to him as a question. He says, "It's too large." Say, "It's too large?" He'll probably say, "Yes, because . . ." and now you know more about the problem you must solve. And/or ask him to rephrase the question or objection — as if you couldn't quite grasp it the first time. At the very least, you will understand his position better. At the very best, he will explain away his own problem while trying to help you understand.

Fourth, if it's appropriate, begin making notes as he talks — *after* you say, "Do you mind if I take a few notes? I don't want to forget anything you say." As you can imagine, this will impress him with your concern, your professionalism, and the esteem in which you hold him and his thoughts. And your notes might even give you the seed of an idea that solves the problem. Imagine that!

Fifth, never forget the value and strength of your basic proven sales presentation. Trust it! There's a reason it covers 97% of your selling situations. It is thorough. It is concise. It is effective. It works! Right? If not, change it immediately! Don't be afraid to rely on it to get you through tough times. More often than not, it is your most reliable asset. If the bomb comes early enough in your presentation, just say, "If you'll bear with me, I really believe I can answer that as we go along — and a lot of other questions you will probably have. O.K.?" You'll almost always get approval if you say it sincerely and, if you can get back on your sales track, your basic presentation will usually either answer it or bury it. And I literally mean it when I say to go back to your basic proven presentation — *including* your standard wrap-up and close, without regard to the bomb he threw. You will be surprised how many times (most!) the subject never again raises its ugly head. It's as if it never happened!

And now the sixth step, what I called the escape hatch earlier. If you have honestly used ALL of the first five steps. If you tried silence. If you tried compliments. If you tried to write your way out of the problem through sincere consultative note-taking. If you fell back on your standard sales presentation and virtually ignored his stated concern. If you truly did all of that and he still has an objection you simply can't handle, then *and only then* say, "Let me be totally blunt. I just don't know the answer. But we have experts who do and I'll be talking with them before the day is over. I'll return tomorrow with the solution — or with an admission that I can't solve it. Tell me exactly what time you want me and the solution to be here." Have your appointment book and pen poised, then *shut up!*

Then win, lose, or draw, be there!

My unicycle-selling friend? He made the sale! How? Simple! He said, "Well, this is a first for me, but I'm a man of my word. If you are willing to try, so am I! Come on up!" There was a pause. The man smiled and said, "Not on your life! I'm not crazy! But I do want one for each of my two kids. Will you let them take my lesson?"

My friend's dynamic tricky close? He said, "You bet!"

The Real
Objection
Is You!

Truman said, "The only thing new in the whole world is the history you don't know." So when a salesperson is stunned with a surprise objection, it tells me that one of two things has occurred. We have either found a salesperson who hasn't studied his product or service enough to know the built-in objections (all products and services have them!) . . . or we have a salesperson who literally carries around his own case of personal objections, infecting everyone he comes in contact with.

Let's take the easy one first.

All products and all services have their own built-in objections. As any true sales professional knows, after he or she has been in the field or on the phone for any length of time, the same basic objections are heard over and over. It may be your price, your quality, your reputation, the size, the color, the shipping time, the view, the speed, the power, the traction, the capacity, the memory, the distance, the condition, the finish, the warranty, or . . . whatever! But each product and each service has its own built-in, absolutely standard, totally predictable objections. It's as if while you were going through sales training school, they were going through prospect objection school!

Your industry, your company, your boss, and your fellow salespeople all hear these same basic objections day in and day out. They are, therefore, able to deal with them effectively — at least the pros are!

These basic built-in objections are so common, so routine, and so expected, I've had salespeople tell me that they are surprised when they hear a "new" objection. In fact, one friend of mine, a woman who makes almost 8,000 telephone presentations a year, told me she doubts she hears more than five new "nonstandard" objections every twelve months!

Therefore, since 95% or more of the objections you have to contend with are to be expected (even welcomed!), there really shouldn't be any major trick involved in preparing yourself to deflect, overcome, and cash in on those objections. It's like playing in the Super Bowl with two evenly matched teams, but your team has both teams' play books! If you think about it, *professional* selling is just about that one-sided!

Are you so new to your company that you don't yet know the standard objections? Ask! And begin keeping a personal log. A pattern will emerge . . . and soon you'll be able to say that you rarely hear new objections, just the same standard run-of-the-mill objections you can easily handle.

This record-keeping habit will also come in handy when you begin to sell a brand new product or model. There will be a few surprises in the beginning, of course. But very quickly the "standard four" objections will emerge and you'll be off and running again — knowing exactly what to expect in almost all sales situations.

But let's get back to the title of this section, _The Real Objection is You!_ That refers to the second type of salesperson I mentioned. The one who is like Typhoid Mary. A living, breathing, walking, talking, disease-carrying sales problem on wheels!

This is the salesperson who hears price objections at the discount buying club. The one who can't sell fax machines because they are too slow. The one who couldn't sell a dating service on a military troop train. This is the one who hears objections no one else ever hears, or hears them out of all proportion to the rest of the industry, the company, and all the other salespeople.

Now understand, we aren't talking about the salespeople who _are_ personally objectionable. That's a whole other problem! We are talking about a disease that can strike any of us without warning. But it is curable if detected early enough!

So what's the problem? The problem is that many among us have the disease and don't know it — because they don't know which objections are standard and which objections are unique to them!

Trust me. If you are the only person who thinks the price is a problem, the price is NOT a problem. Your _personal_ view of the price is the problem!

If no one in the organization but you experiences difficulty with your company's six-week delivery program, the delivery program is NOT the problem. _Your_ perception of six-week deliveries is the problem!

A client of mine sells franchises. They have about fifty

sales representatives across the United States and Canada. Most of their franchises do very well and the people who bought them are generally a happy bunch.

Recently, my client's company was able to lure away a top franchise salesman from another company. Because of his years of experience and success, they neglected to put him through all of the training and indoctrination they usually require. They felt it would be insulting to a man of his stature. Well, you are probably ahead of me, but here's the story.

Instead of taking off like a big bird, he was floundering almost immediately. Instead of breaking all sales records and setting the pace for the rest of the organization, he was quickly becoming an embarrassment to the man who selected him and introduced him with such fanfare — the president of the company!

They asked me to speak to him. I quickly discovered the problem. He was hearing objections he just couldn't overcome. But, as you might have guessed, they were objections almost no one else ever heard in this particular and unique sales organization.

He was hearing the price was too high when, in fact, it was about 15% lower than the industry average. He was hearing that people were afraid they couldn't make enough money in the business when, in fact, the average income of their franchises was about 25% higher than the industry average. And he was hearing that the work involved was too strenuous and demanding when, in fact, the system was so smooth it almost ran itself. So what was really wrong?

Well, it seems that the company he came from *was* overpriced. Their people *were* under-rewarded. And the work involved *was* back-breaking, to say the least! But when he left that company behind, he brought their objections with him into a world where they didn't really exist — or shouldn't have.

How did it happen? My client let him skip the full training experience. He didn't get out "among them." He saw demons where there were none. He saw shadows at high noon. He was snatching defeat from the jaws of victory. HE was the problem!

So keep a careful check on yourself. Understand that most objections are normal, even necessary, for the full sales process to occur. But if you are the only one hearing price objections, it isn't the price — it's you.

I don't really understand how prospects and customers do it, but they have a sixth sense. If YOU doubt the price, so will they. If YOU are embarrassed by your shipping time, they will pick up on it. If YOU think your company should have more or better literature, every prospect you meet will say, "Send me your literature and I'll get back to you."

Remember, after you deal with the standard five, ten, or fifteen objections built into your product, and after you've handled the five or six surprises you should expect each year — after all that is behind you, then all other objections you routinely hear, whatever they may be, were probably brought into the selling situation *by you!*

Your prospects and customers are mirrors of you, your knowledge, your skills, your abilities, and most importantly, your beliefs and convictions. Make sure you like what you see when you look into those mirrors of the mind.

And here's some good news. While it is true you can become the real objection if you aren't careful, it is equally true that you can also be the major *benefit* of dealing with your organization!

The Good-Night Kiss Close

During a conversation with my youngest son last night, I stumbled across a terrific way to explain the art of closing as performed by sales professionals. I won't bore you with the exact conversation Josh and I had, but you'll be able to get the drift of it — at least as it relates to selling.

Picture the typical awkward teenage boy walking the typical awkward teenage girl to her front door after their first date or, depending on your views, their second date. Either way, there they are on the doorstep. The stars are shining — and probably the porch light too! The moon is out. The time is here. Either he gets his good-night kiss or he doesn't. What should he now say to "close the deal"?

65

Stop! Don't answer!

See, if you fell for that trap, we've still got a great deal of work to do! The answer *isn't* what he says now. "Now" is too late! It's what he has said and done from the beginning that counts! From the *very* beginning.

And now you have a glimpse of how the average salesperson views closing sales! Let's look at the average amateur awkward salesperson from the perspective of the average amateur awkward teenage boy.

Our teenage boy (the average, awkward variety) believes many things that are absolutely wrong. He believes he can wait until the last moment, call the young lady in question and say, "You don't want to go to the dance, do you?" He further believes that, once he has found someone stupid enough to say "yes" to that approach, he can show up late and honk the horn for her to come out. Then he'll watch her open her own car door while doing something real cool — like sipping on a beer. Then at breakneck speed, he'll race her to the dance and promptly begin to ignore her while he flirts with the other girls and attempts to out-swear his equally vulgar male friends.

With the dance behind him, he drives her to the local gathering spot. Then, while trying to avoid spending any serious money on her, he wanders around the parking lot — further engaging in juvenile male bonding.

With onions and beer on his breath and body odor to boot, he now races to her house over 45 minutes past her parents' deadline (which he never heard because he didn't bother to meet them). He lets her open her own door, then trails behind her to the front door like an oversexed dog.

Stop the action! Freeze frame the scene!

Let's pull the young boy from the scene and insert an amateur salesman. And let's pull the young girl from the scene and insert a prospective customer. Everything else stays the same.

It is for this *precise moment* in time the poor, amateur, un-skilled, down-at-the-heels salesperson wants me to teach him a "strong close." He wants me to teach him a magic sentence that will overcome all of his transgressions. He wants a short string of words that will compensate for the fact that he is a 24-karat unskilled jerk.

And now for some bad news. Unless he is selling to equally uncouth jerks, or unless he is a deceitful con man, there is no such magic sentence! Just as Diogenes futilely wandered the world looking for an honest man, this poor soul is doomed to wander the sales world looking for the "right job," or the "right close" — never understanding that HE, and HE alone, is the problem!

So how do you avoid the tragic fate of our imaginary friend? You view the sales process and/or the dating process as a complete, unbreakable cycle — a chain, if you will. And you understand that a chain is no stronger than its weakest link! So each link, from the very first to the very last, must be carefully crafted, equally strong, and precisely placed.

But here's the good news. Contrary to what most poverty-stricken salespeople believe, if you will follow the links of the chain concept in selling, the "close" is no longer a mystical and frightening part of the process. It is simply the last of many links — each equally important to the total sale.

So there's nothing to selling after all? Wrong! Selling is the highest-paid profession on earth *because* it's the most diffi-cult profession on earth! Never forget that!

So what's so difficult? Well, try finding honest, ethical people who are willing to learn how to build long, complex, per-fectly formed chains of human relationships for starters! See, that is difficult! But here's the point: Get your eyes off the last link and learn how to build an *entire chain*. Understanding that the very first link, the last link, and every link in between are of equal value. They may not all be equally exciting, but they are equally valuable!

No, you cannot sell if you don't "close the sale." But you also can't sell if you don't prospect, because you won't have anyone to close. And the same is true if you are late, or uninformed, or poorly dressed, or insensitive, or dishonest, or . . .

Get it?

Now back to teenage dating. Let's try it again, but this time the way a professional salesman would handle it if he could somehow disguise himself as a gawky adolescent boy.

First, the prospecting and qualifying. A smart teenager would look over the entire field first. There are many people he would have no interest in and, on the other hand, there are many who would have no possible interest in him. That narrows the field to a manageable number, but it still leaves more than he can ever call on!

Second, with a few highly qualified prospects in mind, he would list them in the order of his preference.

Third, a smart teenager would write down a basic sales presentation and practice it until comfortable.

Fourth, with plenty of time before the planned event, he would call his first choice and give his presentation.

Fifth, assuming he made his first sale to her or to someone on the list, he would begin to plan the actual event.

Sixth, with car washed, teeth brushed, clothes pressed, hair combed, and flowers in hand, he would arrive at her door at the exact time he said he would be there.

Seventh, he would introduce himself politely to her parents, make small talk, and allow them to inspect him.

Eighth, he would escort her to his car, open the door, seat her, close the door, and drive carefully to the event.

Ninth, at the event he would have eyes only for her — as if she was the only person on earth. He would dance with her, get her cokes and snacks, and devote his evening to making hers pleasurable.

Tenth, he would take her to a _special_ place afterwards — not necessarily the local hangout. And there he would continue to be bright and charming, hanging on her every word.

Eleventh, with ten minutes to spare, he would carefully drive her home, all the while telling her what a wonderful evening he'd had.

Twelfth, he would open her car door (having slipped a breath mint into his mouth while circling the car), take her by the hand, and help her from the car.

Thirteenth, continuing to hold her hand, he would slowly walk her to the door while saying he had a great evening and would like to see her again very soon.

Fourteenth, at the door he would gently turn to face her, step slightly closer, and look into her eyes. Then, assuming she hasn't indicated her revulsion for him in some manner, they would _simultaneously_ move towards each other and kiss. Bingo!

See? The kiss is only the logical conclusion to a much longer, well-executed series of events. It isn't a bone-jarring, gear-shifting explosion at the end of a bad meeting.

And once again we have it — the reason why so may top professional salespeople get that funny look on their faces when you ask them for their favorite closes. Many don't understand what you mean. Over the years their sales presentations, and that means all the way from prospecting to closing, have become "seamless." In other words, there isn't an identifiable break in their system. It's all one long unbreakable process.

So the next time you are in a selling situation, remember our young awkward teenage friend. Closing is easy if you take care of all of the other steps along the way first!

★ ★ ★

Save as Much
as You Want

Here's a quick one you may be able to use now or at some point in the future. It's one of those sales and marketing gems that needs to be shared, even if you're *never* able to use it! Just knowing about it may give you the seed for a different idea somewhere down the sales road — an idea that could make you rich!

An associate of mine runs a service company. Too much detail would reveal confidential client information, so let's just say his business is not unlike an insurance company, or a pre-paid road service organization, or a pre-need burial service. By that I mean, while his service is certainly needed and valuable, his expenses are almost nothing unless and until he is called on to perform. And, when compared to his total number of clients, that doesn't happen very often. His business is, therefore, very profitable, to say the least!

Because he hadn't felt any profit pressure to raise his rates, they stayed level for several years. Others in the industry had, however, raised their prices steadily (about 10% a year). End result, after almost eight years, his rates were about half of what his competitors charged.

As you can see, he now had a marketing dilemma. He was making plenty, but only half of what he should have been making. And because he didn't move his old clients along gradually, they faced a real price jolt that would probably cost him a lot of business — even though he was just moving them to the industry norm, and even though they would have to pay at least that much wherever they went!

Further input: Many of his clients were on a month-to-month basis, their original contracts having long since expired.

And more: He is extremely loyal to his clients, so he didn't want to leave anyone in the lurch.

So that's the problem. How do you take a client base of about 1,000 from $125 to $250 per month and make them feel good about it?

Think about it for a moment and see if you can come up with a good solid sales presentation that overcomes all of those problems and challenges. In fact, that's exactly what I was doing with him (thinking about it) when his local friendly bank gave him some additional inspiration!

Seems the construction loan he was getting for his new building wasn't as "surefire" as he'd believed. The bank had discovered that most of his clients were without written agreements. They were month-to-month and could leave at any time. Accordingly, the bank told him they wanted to see signed contracts and would loan against only 50% of the total value of those contracts for the construction loan phase.

A double dilemma! Now he has to go to his clients, double their monthly rates, _and_ tell them that the days of "trust and handshakes" are over — it's signed contracts only from now on!

You might want a few more minutes to think it over. I promise you there's a simple, "make everyone happy" solution to this tremendous sales opportunity! And all the ingredients you need to devise a solution have been given to you.

Once again, here are the basic elements:

1. The business is profitable as is, but he is charging half of what he could and should.

2. Most of his clients are on a month to-month basis — with no contracts.

3. The bank won't loan construction money for his new building without contracts worth at least twice the value of the construction loan.

4. His objectives are to get 100% of his clients on signed contracts, without losing a single client, without discriminating, while doubling his sales volume and, as a result, get his new building financed.

What was your solution? Write to me! I'd love to see yours! Here's what we did: First, we decided to offer our solution to twenty-five of his customers in person as a test. That way, if we were way off base with our brilliant solution, we could withdraw and regroup without destroying his entire business. Or if we met with the enthusiasm we expected, we could write to the rest of them without too much concern.

Second, we made the decision up front that he wasn't going to get all that he wanted — that he would have to compromise on some points (life isn't always exactly as you'd like it!). But we also decided to determine in advance exactly what those compromises would be. In other words, we'd give the clients some predetermined, but absolutely firm, choices (like when you were a child and your mother let you cut the candy bar, but your sister got to pick the piece she wanted).

Here was the final solution:

All literature used to explain the service to clients was immediately revised to show the new higher price. This was done to make it official, firm, and believable to one and all — including some members of his own staff, who were having emotional problems with the change. Nobody likes change!

So, for NEW clients the die was cast on the first day. Good news! There was no more resistance to the new price than there had been to the old! And he offered the clients a benefit he hadn't before. As with your childhood candy bar, it was made clear that there would always have to be a written contract in force, but that the client could pick the length of the contract! In other words, "We'll guarantee to hold the line at $250 per month for as long as your contract calls for, and you get to decide what that is!"

Suddenly, instead of debating month-to-month, six-month or one-year contracts, clients were *demanding* to sign two-year, five-year, and ten-year contracts! For the first time since he began, his business had guaranteed stability! He could literally see his growing income stream years in advance!

As you can imagine, this gave him the courage to sit down with the first of his OLD clients. He was now dealing from a position of strength and confidence!

Oversimplified, here's what he said:

"I've got some good news and some bad news to share with you. As I'm sure you are aware, our rates have lagged behind the rest of our industry for many years. It is now to the point where you are only paying about 50% of what you'd pay anywhere else for the same service, but our quality and reliability are still the very best available.

"To further complicate our problems, we have operated without current contracts with many of our older clients — including you. As you know, that makes financial planning almost impossible. The banks simply can't understand our personal friendship and long-term business relationship!

"Here's the bad news. Effective the first of this month, we increased our monthly rates to $250 and began requiring clients to be on a contract — for their own price protection and for our future financial planning.

"Now here's the good news. We want to work with our old friends. You've been loyal to us and we will continue to be loyal to you. So, if you feel more comfortable without a written agreement, you don't have to have one. We will continue on a month-to month basis with you at the new rate, giving you maximum flexibility. Or, if you'd prefer the stability of a guaranteed rate, protecting you from this price increase and any others that may be necessary in the future, we'll put together a Letter of Agreement at your current rate for any length of time you feel comfortable with — a month, a year, two years, five years, ten years — whatever!

"As you can see, we've designed it so you can choose the option that's best for you — with absolutely no pressure from us. Just like we used to do as kids, we've cut the candy bar, but you get to pick the piece you want!

"Do you want to remain at the old $125 rate or go up to the $250 rate on the first of next month? And, *assuming* you'd prefer to stay at the lower rate, for how long do you want to lock it in?"

What do you think happened? Well, as I told you earlier, with the new customers, he doubled his income immediately and gained stability. As for the existing clients, about 19% of them didn't want to be tied down for any length of time. They agreed to go to the new rate on a month-to-month basis at the beginning of the next month, and their dropout rate percentage average stayed the same as it had always been. So my client doubled his income from this group at no cost in the number of clients — and, almost two years later, it has remained the same, perfectly normal.

And the other 81% of the established clients? They all opted to stay at the lower price, signing contracts up to fifteen years in duration, with an average contract length of six years for this group!

Talk about a win-win-win-win situation! Everyone walked away happy! Old clients are happy! My friend is happy! His bank is happy! And he has moved into his new building — with 100% financing!

And we built in a safeguard for the future, as he didn't want to go through this agony again! His rates are now adjusted January 1st of every year — no more shocks! And all new clients pay whatever the new rate is and sign a contract. And all old clients will pay the prevailing rate when their current contracts expire, along with a new signed contract. Now his business runs like a machine!

As I told you in the beginning of this section, this is one of those bits of sales creativity you just ought to know about! Whether you use all of it, part of it, or just store it away for now, it is what Jimmy Rucker used to call "a stroke"!

Dance With the One
That Brung 'Ya!

T he old Southern saying, "You should dance with the one that brung 'ya," applies to the sales world too — with just a little twist. You should continue to dance with the ones you've already got!

We spend a lot of time on prospecting for and selling to new customers, so we occasionally like to stop and remind ourselves that cultivating and working closely with the customers you already have is *crucial* to long-term success in selling.

Year after year, various reports prove that it is six to ten times more costly to go get a new customer than it is to retain a current one. Six to ten times more expensive!

Does that mean you should stop prospecting for new business? Of course not! Try that and you'll look around one day and find yourself flat broke. Your customer base will always need constant additions. People move away. People die. Companies move away . . . or change direction . . . or go belly up. So you've got to constantly keep adding new customers to your foundation.

But that doesn't change the fact that you can service your existing customers with far less energy and expense than you'll spend chasing after a new account.

And there's a hidden double bonus in this system of working with established customers. Know what it is? Here's a clue: The late, great sales trainer, Elmer Wheeler, was fond of saying, "Find a need and fill it."

Got it now?

If not, here's the answer to the problem and the "need" your customers tell us they want filled. Customer survey after customer survey shows that your customers don't believe you really care about them. They believe you treat them like royalty right up until the sale, then you ride off into the sunset with their money and never look back. And the problem is so severe, many studies show that is the main reason customers stop ordering from one supplier and go to another. Not because of the product, the price, or the quality — just because of you!

Now since we've found a proven customer need, make Elmer Wheeler proud of you and FILL IT!

★ ★ ★

Whatever You Do,
Don't Sell Out

Several of my friends and acquaintances from high school days in Atlanta went on to become rather successful in show business. In fact, two or three of them have become household names.

As a result, I had the opportunity to visit with one of them when he was appearing at Lake Tahoe recently. The popular resort is just up the road from where we live.

I was pleased to see how well he has done and to see that he has handled his wealth, fame, and success gracefully — but I couldn't say the same for a few of his entourage.

If you've ever been around someone with a great deal of wealth or fame, you've probably seen a few of these unfortunate people hanging around. Some are mere flunkies, and they are sad in their own way, but there are also perfectly normal people who provide valuable services for the successful person, and yet too often they fall victim to the flunky syndrome. They somehow surrender the value of their own identity and place their worth in the hands of, and at the whim of, another person.

You've seen them at sales conventions. They laugh too loud when the boss tells a joke. They rarely have a personal opinion on anything, at least not until they've glanced at their leader to try and ascertain his or her feelings first. They run to light cigarettes like trained monkeys, and if the boss is so inclined, they will absorb limitless amounts of personal abuse.

Fortunately for the people around my friend, he isn't inclined to mistreat his staff. But that makes the situation all the more fascinating, because they behave almost the same as those who *are* abused by their bosses. It's almost as if the insecurity comes with the job, or is part of a job description written in a flunky's manual somewhere.

This situation is sad in another way too. You see, my friend and other bosses in his position are ill-served by those who seem to be trying so hard to please them. The "Yes, Boss," "You're right, Boss," "I totally agree, Boss," and "Whatever you say, Boss" mentality cuts off the one thing a person in high position, a person who is already cut off to a certain degree by definition, needs. They need high-quality, absolutely direct, and totally honest input! And that is something a person who has surrendered his or her soul in exchange for being near power and excitement simply can't give.

The message? We probably all need to guard against being in either position — or allowing those around us to be. Surrendering our souls certainly won't get us where we want to go, and being surrounded by people who've surrendered theirs and become mere mirrors and echoes of our own weaknesses is just as bad.

Diogenes, the Greek philosopher, had something to say on the subject. A friend was telling him of the great fortune another man had, having been appointed as Alexander the Great's historian. "What a fortunate man, a part of Alexander's household privileged to be present at his feasts!" he said. But Diogenes replied, "Say rather, how unfortunate a man, who can neither dine nor sup except at Alexander's pleasure."

Diogenes was speaking approximately 300 years before the birth of Christ. Today we have a formalized corporate description of the same situation. We call it the "Golden Handcuffs."

Diogenes left us another lesson in this area of thought when he had this exchange with a fellow philosopher of his day.

The man, who had just obtained an appointment to the court of the ruler of Syracuse, found Diogenes preparing some lentils for a meager meal and said to him, "Diogenes, if you would only learn to compliment him, you wouldn't have to live on lentils." Diogenes replied, "And if you would only learn to live on lentils, you wouldn't have to compliment him."

Fellow salespeople: Maintain, protect, and cherish your dignity.

They Don't Want
Your Product!

One of the most difficult concepts to get across to salespeople is the fact that, with extremely rare exceptions (i.e., a brand new, one-of-a-kind miracle drug available only by prescription), your prospects and customers don't need your product or service. They can get it, something just like it, or something even better, at dozens of places. Probably at hundreds of places. And perhaps for less money.

Want to test the point? The next time you are in some company's Purchasing Department, ask to see their *Thomas Register.* The size of a full set of encyclopedias, it gives sources for just about every conceivable product on earth, complete with names, addresses, and phone numbers. Or just look in the

Yellow Pages or, better yet, the newer selective type of Yellow Pages (Business-to-Business, etc.). See? Your product/service isn't hard to come by. And, now that everyone but your grandmother has a toll-free number, your customers can order from the other side of the country just as easily as from you. And with Federal Express and/or UPS, they can probably get it just as quickly.

Should you just drop out of selling and take that safe, secure job your mother always wanted you to have? Probably not. Read on!

Your customers are looking for more than a product or service. They are looking for solutions to their problems, answers to their questions, something to fill their needs and satisfy their wants, and — get ready for this — someone they can trust!

Note: I said *someone* they can trust. You see, they can buy just your product lots of places, but rarely can they find a source they trust and with whom they feel comfortable. And that's where you come in!

With a good company, and good products or services to back you, and with your own professionalism and integrity fully developed, you are the *only* person on earth who can honestly say, "Mr. Prospect, you can purchase this Lear Jet (or typewriter, computer, car, house, shirt, lot, phone system, etc.) many places. But you should know that only *here* does it come with *me* in the package."

When you can say that proudly and have the customer know that it's good news, then you are off and running!

We've all had bad experiences with large, reputable, successful businesses because our point of contact (the salesperson or the service representative) was not as good as the company. And we've all had good experiences with less-than-perfect companies because the salesperson or representative made up for the faults of the company.

Don't tell me I'm "in good hands with Allstate." That's utter nonsense. Tell me which Allstate representative I'll be dealing with. An associate recently had horrible experiences with both Mazda and Pontiac dealerships, only to have both problems instantly and pleasantly solved by other Mazda and Pontiac dealerships only a few miles apart. In one week, he went from hating Mazda and Pontiac to praising the new dealerships to the skies! He still actively and aggressively steers people away from the first two dealerships, but he has helped sell several cars for each of the second dealerships.

See? It isn't hard to get a Mazda or a Pontiac. They are everywhere and at virtually the same prices, model for model. What *is* hard to find is a quality person standing beside and behind them.

And that's where you and only you can make the difference. That's what professional selling is all about — YOU!

Get Stupid

Some of the best salespeople in the world are often deliberately struck with an outbreak of stupidity. As they will tell you, stupidity can often pay big dividends!

As you know, a very effective method for turning an objection away, or even into an immediate sale, is to have your customer explain the objection in great detail. Especially when it wasn't a valid objection to begin with, this process often results in the customer realizing the objection really wasn't soundly based. Various chapters will give many pointers on how to achieve this reversal with your customers. And I will cover additional techniques in the future. But if you've got a little extra nerve . . . and don't mind putting your ego in your hip pocket occasionally, here's a blockbuster used by many Master Closers around the world.

Similar to the "Old Country Boy" method of selling, the Master Closer is suddenly unable to understand the customer's objection. This doesn't mean you disagree with it — it means you aren't capable of understanding it to begin with! If you really have nerve, you might imply that the customer might just be right — that perhaps you weren't even aware of a major flaw in your product or service. And that puts you in the logical position of being able to ask for even more detail — *far more detail!*

Now this won't work if your customer's objection really is valid. But feigned stupidity is a real objection-killer for handling those that are misconceptions, misunderstandings, the result of a poor sales presentation, or the result of the customer not paying attention to the information he or she has already been given.

A Master Closer who has mastered this technique will lean forward, might look puzzled, perhaps scratch his head, and then respond with a statement or question that *proves* he has missed the customer's point entirely. Usually the customer will try to correct the Master Closer's thinking, which gives you license to say, "I'm sorry. I must be missing something. Please explain it again, slowly. I guess I'm not as bright as I look."

Again, if the objection was invalid, the customer will find it difficult, if not impossible, to explain to you. The result? The objection is explained away by the customer. Or it is clarified, crystallized, and focused into an easy-to-answer specific question. Or, occasionally, you'll get a bonus — the bonus being that the customer realizes the objection was silly and is embarrassed for having raised it. In those situations the customer often is eager to show that HE isn't stupid (even if YOU are!)

and will prove his wisdom by wrapping up the sale himself. That makes him an *Honorary* Master Closer!

This powerful tool must be used carefully, and only in situations where your inability to understand the objection is plausible. It won't work, for instance, in a shoe store if the customer says the shoes are way too small. That's rather clear cut. But most selling situations are far more complicated . . . and many objections are merely poorly thought-out fuzzy generalities designed only to slow the sales process.

A side benefit of this approach is that it rarely, if ever, results in an argument! From your side, you aren't arguing. You are just a little slow on the uptake. From the customer's side, it's very difficult to argue with or get mad at a terribly sincere person who is just trying desperately and empathetically to understand.

Despite what your parents, teachers, and bosses have told you over the years, sometimes stupidity DOES pay!

Study Robin Hood

An old friend, Jane Ferguson of Atlanta, Georgia, asked that we once again cover a point that all salespeople need to remind themselves of from time to time. A popular seminar leader and sales trainer used to call it the "Robin Hood Program."

His point, made humorously, was that he had studied Robin Hood's career, discovering that, besides any charitable purpose, Robin stole only from the rich because the poor didn't have anything worth taking!

Think about it. Had Robin Hood stolen from the poor and given to the rich, he and his merry band of followers would soon have gone out of business.

Transferred to the sales world, the lesson is simple. Spend your time working with customers who have the *means* to buy your product or service. You see, many people who hear your presentation would love to buy — but they simply don't have the money!

As a professional salesperson, it is your job to determine your customer's financial ability in advance whenever possible. Failing that, it is your job to determine it as early in the sales interview as humanly possible. Then, when a lack of ability to buy is discovered and confirmed, it is your job to cut your losses quickly. Your time is best spent with people who have the financial wherewithal to take action.

All salespeople step into this trap occasionally, but there are three types in selling who do it constantly! See how you and your associates score.

First, there is the amateur salesperson. Although he/she may have been "selling" for 30 years, they still haven't developed the professional instincts and skills needed to tie down a prospect as to his/her financial qualifications to buy. As a result, they are always the "also rans" in their sales office.

Second, there is the fearful, overpolite, fainthearted salesperson. This type knows intellectually that prospects must be individually financially qualified, but simply lacks the nerve to do it. They never make it to the top in selling because, like the kid who is afraid of the cold water in the swimming pool, they never take the plunge. They never give themselves the opportunity to adjust to the concept, to get comfortable with it.

Last, and by far the worst type, we have the salespeople who are actually grateful to spend their time with the totally unqualified and morbidly curious. You see, they fear rejection so much that they feel safe and warm only with people who can't possibly buy. Unqualified, financially embarrassed prospects are generally wonderful conversationalists. They can relax and chat for hours because they have absolutely nothing to fear from The Closer — secretly knowing they couldn't buy if they had to!

Want to know where the approximately 70% yearly turn-over we experience in selling comes from? Well, a huge percentage of it comes from these three types of salespeople — the Amateur, the Fearful, and the Grateful. Here's a mental trick to help you assume the role of a good qualifier. Early in the sales process, picture yourself as a doctor, lawyer, or loan officer. As you know, these people seem to have no problem when asking us pointed, probing questions. And because of their professionalism, their displayed concern for us, and their obvious need to have the facts, we don't mind giving them the information. Would you want to be treated by a doctor who didn't "qualify" you? Of course not. And neither do your customers. In fact, when done properly, they actually appreciate being qualified!

Picture this. You walk onto a used car lot. You have $8,500 maximum to spend and the salesperson tries to sell you a two-year-old Rolls Royce. See the embarrassing position that puts you in? Or worse yet, he takes one look at you, asks no questions, and leads you over to the $500 junkers!

What if he had spent just a few moments with you discussing what you were trying to accomplish with your purchase and how much money you had to work with? Wouldn't that be better for both of you? Of course!

Last, but not least, like Robin Hood, work with more and more qualified prospects all of the time. Deliberately put yourself in positions to deal with and associate with the folks who have the cash to act. Remember, you can sell more widgets at the country club accidentally than you can with closing skills on skid row!

Perot's Secret

H. Ross Perot will probably go down in history as one of the greatest salespeople who ever lived. And as a man who some have said is the second wealthiest person in America, he certainly would be considered a successful businessperson. From a superstar salesperson at IBM to the founder of Electronic Data Systems, he has blazed a trail across the history of business throughout the world.

I've often wondered what makes one person as successful as Ross Perot, while another person, with seemingly equal or greater talent, does little by comparison.

Well, I don't have all of the answers to that riddle and I

doubt that Ross Perot does either — but if you'd like some insight into his personality and attitude, here are some thoughts directly from Mr. Perot:

On job security:
Get up in the morning and look in the mirror. You are your own job security.

On building a team:
I was dead interested in getting beyond talk and getting down to action. Now the first thing you've got to do in a company the size of General Motors, or any other company, is tap the full potential of the people. If the people are all divided up and fighting, you're never going to do that. You've got to build a single unified team. In order to do that you've got to build trust and respect right down on the factory floor. You've got to earn the loyalty of the people.

On failures:
Failures are skinned knees — painful but superficial.

On who makes policy:
It's kind of hard to forget 800,000 people. It's awfully hard to forget those folks who work in the factories. We've got this crazy phenomenon all across big business in this country — every time we have a problem we want to blame the people on the factory floor. Now with a sports team, the people would laugh you off the field. If the team can't win, you blame the coach.

On our society:
Our country is so big and complex that people turn the switches off. Apathy is our greatest national weakness.

On fundamentals:
The most fundamental things don't cost money. You don't have to spend a billion dollars to start treating people with respect, you don't have to spend a billion dollars to provide true leadership.

On entrepreneurial spirit vs. mega-management:
I don't believe that treating people with dignity and respect, tapping their ideas, focusing all of the energy of an 800,000-person organization on one thing — making a great car — is entrepreneurial. I just think that's plain good business.

On company philosophy:
The car capital of the world is Toyota City — not Detroit. The company philosophy is, "Every employee is a brother." That's what we have to have.

On his struggle with GM's Board of Directors:
You know there are a lot of ways to fight — you don't always fight the same way — sometimes use bottles, sometimes use knives, other times just kick 'em in the shins.

On success:
A person is never more on trial than in a moment of excessive good fortune.

On quotas:
There was a time when I identified with Thoreau's line about the mass of men living lives of quiet desperation. I was working as an IBM salesman and they put a quota on the amount I could earn. [In the first nineteen days of 1962 Perot exceeded his entire year's quota.]

On EDS's beginnings:
Our biggest assets were our dreams.

On hometown expense accounts:
I haven't sold anybody over lunch in my whole life. There's nothing worse than driving a point home when a guy's fiddling with his salad.

On the status quo:
If it doesn't make sense, change it!

On activism:
An activist is the guy who cleans up the river, not the guy who concludes that it is dirty.

On education:
Our education does not develop leadership. Our focus has got to be on the development of people, not gadgets.

On family:
If I could do one thing, I would try to construct a strong family unit for every family on the basis of love, understanding, and encouragement.

On ideas:
Ideas are precious and fragile things and it's terribly important that we encourage them.

Taken individually, none of those ideas sound earth-shaking. In fact, taken as a whole, we've all heard most of them before — in one form or another. So why is Ross Perot's success so outstanding? Maybe because he didn't just talk about these ideas, he put them into action on a daily basis — and billions of dollars flowed to him as a perfectly natural result. Just a by-product of successful living.

Conditions versus Objections

This particular chapter may not help you close many more sales — if any. But it might just keep you out of the salespersons' mental ward.

Here's an absolute fact: You will never be able to close every sale you attempt. NEVER. The only people who appear to do that are order-takers working in situations where the customer would buy the product in spite of the order-taker (i.e., grocery store clerks, gas jockeys, fast food clerks, etc.). The rest of us are going to face setbacks on a regular basis.

Many sales managers don't want to even open the door to the possibility of it being O.K. for you to miss a sale. They are afraid, and with some justification, that it is a short hop from their excusing your failure in one selling situation to your excusing your failure in all selling situations. And it's not that hard to see how they got to thinking that way, is it?

Well, I'm not your sales manager, so I can speak the unspeakable. I can help you understand that there are simply times when a sale can't and shouldn't be made.

"I can't afford it," sometimes really means, "I can afford it, but you haven't yet explained the benefits to me in such a manner that I feel good about exchanging my hard-earned cash for your product." In that situation, "I can't afford it" is an overcomable objection . . . and a Master Closer will clarify his or her product's benefits so clearly that the customer will virtually demand that the "cash for product" exchange takes place.

On the other hand, sometimes "I can't afford it" means "I can't afford it." Strange, but true! And in that situation, you don't have an **objection,** you have a **condition,** and there is probably nothing you can do about it. At least for the time being.

Never forget, however, that situations will always change. The person who can't afford your product today, or has no real need or want for it now, will probably be in a different situation at some point in the future. And these unqualified prospects can also often be wonderful sources of leads — qualified people who can afford your product.

You will quickly drive yourself into another career if you become emotionally distraught every time a customer says "no," but you'll get there even faster if you count the real misses with the ones you never had a shot at. As in baseball, balls and strikes should be counted differently.

We have a client that sells a very popular and powerful package. Everything in the package is something their properly qualified prospects would want to own. The components of the package have an honest-to-goodness retail value of about $600, but their customers are offered the entire package for about 80% off of the retail value if they take it the first time it is offered to them. It is a very strong introductory offer to say the least!

Here's how they finally got their salespeople to understand conditions versus objections. As a survey sample, they took 1,000 orders in a row. They discovered that 80% of the people who heard the details of the package bought it immediately, but that 20% said "no." So they ran test approvals on the credit cards of the 20% for the full amount of the package (versus the smaller step-down order that was actually placed). They didn't charge the customers! They just tested to see if the higher amount would have cleared. Guess what? Of the 200 people who said "no," 160 of them had to — they simply didn't have the money! It was their own personal **condition.** It was not an **objection** at all!

Here's a bonus lesson from the experiment. Though it's somewhat off the point, it is important nonetheless. Our client's salespeople then gave the 40 remaining customers (the ones who said "no" but DID have the money) another sales presentation and another opportunity to take the package. Results? 80% of them took it! That was 32 additional sales!

End result? They only missed 168 people out of 1,000, and 160 of them weren't financially qualified to begin with!

A true story? YOU know it is! Almost every single reader of this book has had that exact same presentation made to him/her. Many of you took it immediately (about 80%). Some of you didn't (about 20%). And now you know why the salespeople didn't take it personally if you said "no."

Now I hope you can better understand the difference between a **condition** and an **objection.**

★ ★ ★

Guarantee It!

Years ago a young salesman worked for a department store in Atlanta, Georgia. It was called Davison's (now Macy's). It was an excellent chain of stores with a wide variety of competitively priced, high-quality merchandise. The buying power of the Macy's chain gave it what should have been a significant edge over its arch-rival, a locally owned department store called Rich's. They bought from the same vendors, they ran virtually the same ads, they matched each other almost store for store, sharing many of the same shopping centers. Their main stores were only a few blocks apart on world-famous Peachtree Street.

So why was Rich's Atlanta's favorite store by far? And why did our young friend have trouble getting even his own family to shop at Davison's?

It was because of Rich's famous guarantee and because of the legendary "Window."

Their guarantee was simple: *"If you are ever, for any reason, dissatisfied with a purchase made at Rich's, bring it back for a complete, no-questions-asked refund — GUARAN-TEED!"*

Their "Window" was even more powerful. It was a large display window right on Peachtree Street. In it were displayed some of their more interesting returned items — all of which had received a 100% refund. Two items in particular that our young salesman recalled in later years were:

1. A pair of high-button shoes that a family had returned when their elderly grandmother died. The shoes had never been worn, but they had been purchased sixty years before they were returned!

2. A broken steam iron that had actually been purchased at another store. Rich's exchanged it for a brand new Rich's AMC iron just to make their customer happy. The type of steam iron? The returned iron's label, shining proudly in Rich's display window lights, clearly showed it was a Macy's private label iron!

The truth was that Macy's had the same guarantee, but you couldn't have convinced anyone of that fact. Rich's advertised their guarantee heavily, they bragged about it, they issued press releases whenever a particularly interesting item was returned. They shouted it from the rooftops! And whenever our young salesman asked his mother to shop his store, she'd always reply that she'd feel better at Rich's — "just in case I have to return it."

How you adapt or adopt this powerful guarantee to your particular product or service is up to you, but do it ASAP! Fortunes are being made all over the world by appealing to the basic need your customers have to be reassured that everything will be exactly as you said it would.

Federal Express gets it there on time or you don't pay. Domino's delivers the pizza on time or gives you money back off the price . . . and if you still aren't happy, it's free! "50,000 miles or 5 years — guaranteed," said Iacocca, and he was selling cars nobody wanted, while in bankruptcy!

Here's a guarantee you may use as a model. See how close you can get to it. It's from our own publishing house, Hampton Books: *"We offer a lifetime, unconditional, no-questions-asked, money-back guarantee on every book, audio cassette, and video we sell. If you are ever dissatisfied with anything you receive from Hampton Books, for any reason, return it for an immediate, cheerful, 100% refund."*

Think you could sell a little more with a guarantee like that backing you up? You betcha!

Power Closers
Listen Clearly!

Those of us who have the honor, privilege, and responsibility of directing the activities of others, and that certainly includes sales professionals, need to develop a special sense: the ability to hear the unspoken — the cry for help that many of our people understate, mask entirely, and sometimes deny they made.

A friend of mine, Danny Cox, used to give a seminar entitled *"Your People Get Better Right After You Do."* One of the points he made was that among a manager's responsibilities was the requirement to listen carefully for even the most subtle of messages coming from your business team.

I know I've discovered that people often say one thing and mean another. That a person who says he isn't interested in trophies usually wants recognition even more than the lady who admits openly that she works only for awards. That the person who says sales training is a joke is often pleading for special help and assistance in his/her sales career.

One of my early mentors told me to listen to what people **meant,** which usually had little or nothing to do with the words they were **saying.** That was a hard one for me to learn, but with lots of practice I've found that it can become an art, or maybe even a science. If you make a game of it, perfecting your newly acquired skill can be a lot of fun and terribly interesting.

When we become really sensitive, even the words being used become less important. We can operate mainly on the feelings we pick up from others.

I have a friend who is so good at this, he takes a tour of his entire office building every day, usually first thing in the morning. Although he appears to be simply greeting each person, he is actually taking their emotional temperatures person by person. I've seen him in action, and the slightest change from normal behavior — and I mean the slightest — by any single person, registers with him like a fire alarm bell.

I asked him if he was born with this talent and he assured me it was a trained skill. A skill that could be learned by anyone. He calls the skill . . . *caring.*

Want to know when he decided to pick up this wonderful talent? It seems that years ago a series of personal setbacks sent my friend to the very brink of suicide. Not really wanting to make the final trip, he said that he sent out *dozens* of subtle, hidden cries for help to his boss, a man he respected greatly. The boss, however, failed to pick up the messages and my friend almost went over the edge. In fact, only a chance meeting with a super-sensitive stranger at a social gathering finally saved him. It seems that the stranger cared and was tuned in to those around him — really tuned in.

Just minutes after my friend and the man met, this person said to him, "I almost took my own life a few years ago, and YOU are thinking about it now. Want to talk about it?"

In the wink of an eye, from a total stranger, my friend's life was literally saved.

Was that what turned my friend into a super-sensitive? You'd think so, but it wasn't. It actually occurred quite some time afterwards when a friend of his committed suicide. Sitting at his friend's funeral, half-listening to the minister drone on, he thought of the many times his friend had called out to him. Not directly. In subtle ways. But he hadn't been *listening,* hadn't been *feeling* like he should have been. Not even as much as a perfect stranger had been at a party years before. So that's when he began to change — at his friend's funeral.

I guess you could say "Better late than never," but that won't bring back the friend.

I thought of all this when I read a humorous but true story about the Australian explorer, Sir Edgeworth David, and his assistant, Douglas Mawson. Seems that Mawson was busy in his tent when he heard Sir Edgeworth call out, "Are you very busy?"

"Yes, I am. What's the matter?" he replied.

"Are you really very busy?" the voice said with a little more urgency.

"Yes," snapped Mawson. "What is it you want?"

There was a moment's silence and then the voice came again, this time apologetically. "Well, I've fallen down in a crevasse and I don't think I can hang on much longer."

You see, some of our people may also be down in a crevasse and some of them are losing their grasps too. Let's listen to them carefully.

My friend's name? Read David Niven's book, *Bring on the Empty Horses.* You'll find the answer to the mystery, or at least the formula for solving it, and you'll really enjoy the book.

Become an Expert

We have for years advocated Consultative Selling, or what we call Power Selling. It means, among other things, becoming a recognized expert in your field.

Selling real estate could be a good example. If, as a licensed Realtor, you can sell literally any property in your area, and if you know your area well, then you are on your way to Consultative/Power Selling. Why? Because you automatically have the position of impartiality. In other words, if you learn to control your client and develop your selling skills, you win no matter what property your prospect purchases. It simply gives you the flexibility of relaxing and working with your clients instead of against them.

The concept of Consultative/Power Selling is less easy to understand in some other industries. How, for instance, can you take this "power position" if you are selling Lincolns with a Cadillac dealership right down the street? Or what if you are selling jewelry and there are three other jewelers within walking distance? Or cosmetics? Or investments? Or cookware? Or timeshares? Or land? Or memberships?

Good news! It's just as easy as real estate, with a lot less driving around!

You just need to become a recognized expert in your field. Not just in your product or service, but in your entire field or industry.

Why would the prospect want to go see competitive products after visiting with you? Well, besides the fact that you didn't close the sale to begin with, they go visit your competitors to see what they have to offer. But what if YOU could explain what they have, in a totally objective manner, and then explain why you, as an expert, decided to work with the company and product you selected?

"Mr. Prospect, I can see why you'd be interested in also looking at the Cadillac line. I faced the same decision regarding my entire career just a few years ago, and I review my decision once a year, when the new models come out. Let me assure you that the first year they make a line of cars superior to Lincoln, I'll go down the street with you!

"Mr. Prospect, I've really done my homework. In fact, I'm considered to be somewhat of an expert in the automobile business. Sit down and let me share some of the things I've found out the hard way. Then, when we're through, if you think a Cadillac is best for you, I'll drive you down there, introduce you to the sales manager, and make sure you're treated properly."

Do you have the courage to handle your customers that way? Well, it doesn't take courage if you are backed up by knowledge. How do you get your knowledge? You must subscribe to and read all of the trade journals that your industry has to offer. Study your competition to the point that you know their products as well as you know your own — maybe even better. Join your trade associations. Go to the meetings and seminars. Become the person other people automatically come to when they want the inside scoop on your type of product.

How long will it take you? Just for starters, how about giving it one solid hour a day over the next year? That's the equivalent of forty-six solid eight-hour days of study, or about a month and a half's worth. And let me assure you, that's a month and a half more study than 99% of your competition will put in over the next twelve months. In fact, it's more than 80% of your competition will put in the rest of their lives!

Our old friend, the late Earl Nightingale, used to say, "If you have a secret, write a book. Then place a copy in every library in the United States. Your secret will be safe." Well, safe from your competitors maybe, but not from you. Not anymore!

Closers
Communicate
Clearly

As I think you suspected by now, I love things that are well said and unmistakably clear. This is a trait all sales professionals must develop. Here's a little gem that fits that category and it is an excellent measure to use when we are checking our own clarity and, in this case, commitment to our own beliefs.

In addition to serving as a member of the House of Representatives, Governor of Massachusetts, Ambassador to England, and Secretary of State, Edward Everett was an orator of great repute. He was also president of Harvard University from 1846 to 1849, and it was there that he placed himself among the all-time best at making himself and his point clear.

It seems that a political and social storm had arisen over the proposed admission of a young black student to Harvard's freshman class. Everett responded, "If this boy passes the examination he will be admitted, and if all of the white students choose to withdraw, all of the income of the college will be devoted to HIS education."

It doesn't leave a lot of room for doubt or misunderstanding, does it? Try it in your sales presentations.

The Better Resolution

Because your customers don't know your products or services as well as you do, they frequently don't ask the right questions. As a result, what they think they want and what they really need are often in conflict.

What should you, the professional salesperson, do when this conflict arises? Should you let the customer buy what he thinks he needs just to get the sale? Or should you jeopardize the entire sale by trying to redirect him to the product or service that will provide the real benefit he wants?

Because of the way the questions are phrased, the proper and ethical answer is evident. But how do you do that out in the real world, while trying to put the kids through college?

First, remember that the true sales professional always takes the long view and does what is best for the customer. As in *The Closers:* "Sum Tertius" (I am Third, after God and the other fellow). Because, and in addition to the obvious moral question, when he discovers the error (and he always will), he will blame it on you, as well he should!

The solution?

Suggest that he simply consider an optional course of action. Don't forget that you are a counselor. You are on his side. Together, slowly discover that there is an even better alternative! While his solution was certainly good (customers are never wrong, even when they are), the two of you have been able to "improve" it.

Done properly, your customer will welcome the new answer to his problem because he worked it out with you — a recognized expert in the field. And he really did make the final decision, because you let him compare the original solution with the new solution, coming to the obvious answer on his own — or so you allow him to think.

Now you must solidify the deal by congratulating him on his wise decision. Give him full credit for having been wise enough to see the proper way to gain the benefits he was seeking. He is, indeed, a very smart businessperson!

By the way, this teamwork approach to selling is absolutely critical if the better solution is priced higher than his original choice. If it wasn't his idea to change his mind, he might assume you were just trying to bump his order up for a fatter commission check.

So the next time one of your customers makes an error in judgment, don't just take the order and run. And resist the temptation to show him that you are right and he is stupid. Simply guide him, ever so gently, to a much wiser course of action.

Handling Sales
Rejection

One of my client friends says in his sales training seminars that there are only two valid reasons to be in selling. You're either good and love the money, or you're bad and you love rejection!

Oversimplified perhaps, but there is some real truth in it.

Selling is said to be the highest paid profession on earth, when properly practiced by professionals. And, since the law of supply and demand always sets prices in a free market, one would have to ask, "Why is it the highest paid?" The answer being, it's the most difficult profession on earth to perform at a professional level over a sustained period of time.

O.K., if it pays so well, why do some sales industries have over a 90% yearly turnover? And why is it that almost 70% of the people in sales this year won't be selling two years from now? REJECTION!

From our first conscious thoughts as young children, we've wanted to be loved, approved of, agreed with, wanted, needed, and to have people say "yes" to our every single request. It is basic to human nature. But in professional selling, the vast majority of us hear "no" far more than we ever hear "yes." Far more times.

So, besides improving our sales skills, product/benefit knowledge, and people skills — all of which would greatly reduce the number of times we hear "no" — what should we do?

Here are some tips.

First, always try to leave a selling situation with at least some small victory. If only for a future appointment. Perhaps even a small sample order, or a commitment to just try your product or service on a test basis.

Second, never leave the interview until you've discovered the real reason the prospect said "no." You may not want to hear it, but you can't solve the problem until you know what it is — with this prospect and/or with others in the future.

Third, don't take the rejection personally, unless of course, you are a personally objectionable character! The "no" probably wasn't meant to insult you. It was directed at your product or service, its price, the delivery time, or some other factor. Or perhaps you were dealing with an unqualified prospect, financially or otherwise.

Finally, ask yourself how many times you've said "no" to other salespeople in the last year. In those situations, were you telling the salespeople you couldn't stand them? Or were you really just saying that their product or service simply didn't fill your needs at the time?

To go a step further, how many times have we all made a purchase in spite of the salesperson, refusing to let him or her stand between us and the benefit we were seeking?

Folks, rejection ain't easy but, when you consider what they pay us to take it, it's sure better than any alternative we can think of!

I Know Just How You Feel

O ur old friend Larry Wilson started a selling craze in the 1960s with a wonderful selling phrase for overcoming objections that were based on false assumptions. The problem was the phrase became so popular every salesperson in the world used it and it wore itself out. By 1975, salespeople even reported trying to use it, only to have their customers feed it back to them, word for word!

Good news! The people who only use the latest in "fad closes" have long since gone on to use other trendy buzzwords, so it's once again safe for the true sales professional to return to one of the all-time great devices. It's called **"Feel, Felt, Found"** and, if you aren't already using it, this one idea should pay for the cost of this book one hundred times over.

Here's how it works:

Your customer has just expressed an objection or concern based on wrong information or on an incorrect impression of your product or service. (Each of you can fill in that blank for yourself, as each of you has at least one such misconception built into your product or service.) For instance, if you are selling Audis, we all know a major problem you face with each and every customer. Right? O.K., now think of your product's built-in, but incorrect objections.

When the customer voices this concern, the natural human tendency is to dispute him/her. "No, Mr. Prospect, you are totally wrong on that point. Here's the truth, you poor misguided fool."

Perhaps you can *sense* the problem that approach creates in your relationship with the prospect! And the same is true for all of the milder, more subtle versions of that same approach. You see, no matter how kind you are, you wind up telling the prospects that they are dead wrong. Stupid might be another term.

Try this instead: *"Mr. Prospect, I know exactly how you* ***FEEL***. *In fact, that's exactly the way I* ***FELT***, *until I was able to gather some additional information. Would you like to know what I* ***FOUND***?"

Of course he would! No one wants to remain an ignorant fool forever! The result? You told him he was wrong, but without telling him he was wrong. And you told him that he wasn't alone, that you too were ignorant of the facts in the past. Then you shared new information with him, information that allowed him to gracefully join the more *enlightened* team — yours!

This works equally well with third-party selling. For example: *"Mr. Prospect, I know exactly how you* ***FEEL***. *In fact, that's exactly the way your neighbor, Bob Brighter,* ***FELT*** *until just recently. Would you like to know what he **FOUND**?"* Of course he would! He doesn't want his neighbor to be smarter than he is.

So the customer turns to the Audi saleswoman and says, "I really like the looks of the car, but I don't think I want to risk my family's lives by buying them a rocket sled. I just saw the *60 Minutes* report, you know."

What do you do? Run? Hide? Cry? Offer him a free matching crash helmet? Try this: *"Mr. Prospect, I know exactly how you **FEEL**. In fact, I **FELT** exactly the same way about Audis when I was considering whether to join the Audi team. Would you like to know what I **FOUND**?"*

Of course he would! And he obviously didn't know that Audi was totally absolved of ANY mechanical problems related to sudden acceleration by a major U.S. Government study and report (that received far less publicity than did the original sensational headlines!). The story he saw was wrong and you have the proof! But you have to "grease" the information for him.

You see, that's what you are PAID to do. Take on the hard ones — head up. But with **FEEL, FELT, FOUND** working for you, it's a heck of a lot easier!

FEEL, FELT, FOUND is absolute magic!

Here's How to Show Your Benefits

I am forever hammering on selling the benefits of your product/service. But a letter we received from a young lady new to selling said in part, "But how do I show my product's benefits? Is there a format, or do I just go through them like a laundry list?" Good question!

Simply reciting the general benefits of your product probably won't do the trick, so here are a few tips to make your product's benefits clear, understandable, meaningful, and exciting to your prospect.

First and foremost, you must determine what your product's benefits are to *your customer.* Not to the last customer. Not to the next customer. To the customer at hand — exclusively. Remember, he couldn't care less how it benefits someone else. He is only interested in what you and your product/service can do for him! So you must review your product's total list of benefits, selecting only those that are meaningful to *each individual* customer!

Next, with his personal list of benefits in front of you, prioritize them in order of importance to him. You do this because you will want to spend most of your time and energy, or your main selling effort, elaborating those points fully.

How do you know which benefits are most important to him? Research and common sense. Your experience with others similar to him. And (make sure you're sitting down for this one) ASK HIM!

On that last point, here's a goal for you. When you are really strong and confident as a Master Closer, do what one of our good friends does. He hands his customer a list of ALL of his product's benefits and a red pen. Then he asks the customer to help him give a meaningful sales presentation by checking off only the benefits he really wants to hear more about. Then he asks the customer to number them in the order of importance to him. And then, using the list the customer created, he gives his sales presentation accordingly. It works wonders!

Now make sure that you understand this about any benefit you explain to a customer. He must be told the "reasons why" these benefits will be obtained. You can tell him your product will improve his bowling league average, but if you don't tell him why it will, he probably won't believe you.

How do you get to know the "reasons why"? Make another list! As you'll recall from other sales tips and techniques, you must convert each of your product's features into benefits. And now you know to make a *prioritized* list of those benefits for each customer. So now you need to put a matching "reason why" next to each and every benefit!

Get it? Your product has features. You must convert them to benefits. And those benefits must be converted to believability by you through "reasons why." Simple, huh?

Last, but not least, develop and/or work with your company to develop offers that are so "benefit-loaded" and "why-justified" that they are hard to resist. Try discounts, special introductory offers, free trials, extra bonuses, free bonuses for ordering now, flexible payment options to credit-worthy customers, free gifts of related items, strong guarantees (lifetime guarantees if you can possibly do it!), etc., etc.!

The Grand Canyon Response

An old sales pro in North Carolina, and a good friend of many of our staff, is known as "Mr. Echo." His favorite response to a tough question is what he calls his "Grand Canyon Response." We've all heard salespeople use this basic technique to one degree or another, but he is the Grand Master of *"Echo Salesmanship."*

To understand how his technique got its name, picture your prospect standing at the edge of the Grand Canyon. He yells, "Your price is too high!" Without fail, the Grand Canyon responds, "Your price is too high!" The prospect yells, "Your delivery is too slow!" and the Grand Canyon responds, "Your delivery is too slow!" It works every time!

All Mr. Echo does is turn the echo into a question when he takes the place of the Grand Canyon, and then Mr. Echo has the courage to shut up. The prospect says, "I don't like the color." Mr. Echo says, ***"You don't like the color?"*** and then stares at the prospect! Until finally, the customer explains what he means. And that frequently means he'd be happy to take the same car (or whatever), but in red. And Mr. Echo doesn't have to go through the whole rainbow guessing the possible colors.

"It's too big." ***"It's too big?"***

"It's too small." ***"It's too small?"***

"I can't wait that long." ***"You can't wait that long?"***

Not only does it force your customer to tell you what's too big, too small, too slow, or too green — thereby easing your job considerably — but it keeps YOU in control of the conversation. Remember, in selling, the person who asked the last question is in control of the conversation and, therefore, the sales process. As J. Douglas Edwards used to say, "Whenever you're in trouble, ask a question!"

Those who've been honored to go out on sales calls with Mr. Echo will tell you it can be an unnerving experience. If you aren't used to this particular approach, you'd feel like saying, "He just said that!" Or, "Can't you hear? He said it was priced too high! Answer him!" But Mr. Echo won't be deterred. He says that most people don't really mean what they say when they voice objections. They are just blurting out what they learned when they went to Customer University, the school of objections. And when forced to explain their objections, they usually resolve them all by themselves!

Under Mr. Echo's program, this unique style gives him the opportunity to save his time, talent, and energy for the really tough questions! And that's what he really gets paid for!

Watch Your Mouth

A large seminar business has sprung up in this country teaching businesspeople how to chew with their mouths closed. Although it covers other social graces, basically that's it. Apparently we have raised a generation of people who have learned their exquisite table manners from drive-thru windows at McDonald's and various other top-of-the-line dining establishments.

Well, if you are looking for a way to get rich, here's a similar market just waiting for the right person. Teaching salespeople how to speak and write properly, to use a full and effective vocabulary, and to utilize the manners their parents should have taught them. Sure, they could go to a community college and take excellent English classes from highly qualified instructors, but that looks far too much like work. What this country is ready for is a training company with a cute name that helps people NOT to sound like unschooled bimbos. And unfortunately, it sounds like we've raised a generation of them too!

You'll have to name the company yourself, but when you're ready, the first market to go after is salespeople. Here's an entire industry full of people who can't utter three sentences in a row without making a major error in grammar. And to make matters worse, they seem to have extremely limited vocabularies.

Here's what to teach them:

The language they use is a major factor in how people view them. It is one of the most important ways they convey, or fail to convey, their professionalism.

Their speech, vocabulary, and grammar must be AT LEAST equal to that of the customers with whom they work.

They must not only have a full general vocabulary, but also the vocabulary of their own industry.

Their vocabulary must be broad enough to relate to all of their customers, from the most uneducated person to the most educated and sophisticated. People will always feel more comfortable dealing with someone on their own level — whatever that level may be.

Their vocabulary should be effective, clear, and to the point. They shouldn't sound too formal, or as if they are reading a script, nor so casual and breezy that they aren't taken seriously.

Tell them to drop several words from their vocabulary, including all profanity (cuss words) and that fabulous phrase, "You know?"

Tell them to get a copy of *Roget's Thesaurus* and begin enlarging their vocabularies TODAY!

Tell them to invest in a tape recorder, so they can record

themselves. Then they can begin to work on tone, speed of delivery, and emphasis.

Tell them that Dizzy Dean and Yogi Berra made it to the top in spite of bad grammar — but that they were both good and colorful baseball players. The rest of us need to learn how to communicate.

Better late than never, you know?

Your Switchboard
Is Killing You!

Many of you are making less than you ought to. Many of you are living well beneath your potential living standard. Many of you don't dress as well, eat as well, or drive as well as you ought to. Why? Because a substantial portion of your sales are killed before they ever get to you. They're viciously murdered by your Killer Switchboard.

For years, I've maintained that the two most important groups of people in most organizations are the ones who answer the phone and the ones who deliver or ship the product or service. That's because they are able to form the image of you and your company even better than you can. They make the very first impression and the very last impression on many of your customers.

As I said, I've felt this for a long time, but it was really driven home the other day. I was working with some top-notch sales executives, people who spend a great deal of time on the phone calling other fellow salespeople.

They were telling me about the rapidly sinking quality level of people who answer the phones in the sales organizations they call in the course of a sales day. They carried on so much that I agreed to spend one full day in their office calling typical client companies. All I had to do was make the initial call and ask for the salesperson by name.

Understand, I knew that telephone receptionists/secretaries/switchboard operators had been killing sales *occasionally* for years. In fact, I was lecturing on the subject long before the telephone became the dominant sales tool it is today. That said, let me tell you I was totally unprepared for the lesson I learned in the course of eight hours and 127 phone calls.

Let me make the setting clear for you: I was calling from a highly regarded company. I was calling people who wanted to be called. In fact, in many cases I was returning their phone calls. And the person answering the phone didn't know if I was a customer, family member, doctor or salesperson . . . at least not at first.

Folks, with a few notable exceptions, they are killing you!

In larger organizations, they frequently don't even know who you are or seem to care. They act as if they have never heard of you. They answer the phone and announce their company so abruptly that the caller isn't sure who he or she called. They are rude. They pop gum in your ear, unless it is lunchtime, in which case they can be heard chewing food. The "you're-interrupting-my-day" attitude that was once the signature of a New York operator has now spread across the country, even into the last stronghold of charm and manners, the deep South.

I suggest you call your own company and ask for yourself! And do it at least once a week, especially if a new person begins answering your phone.

This isn't just a good idea or something to think about. Get it handled quickly! The best closer in the world would have a tough time succeeding if first his or her customers talked to many of the people I chatted with on that horrible day!

Please understand, I talked to several people who were absolutely wonderful. They are, or should be, full partners in your sales efforts. Every sale you ever make is due, in large part, to them and the first impression they make. However, they made up only about 5% of all the people I talked to. Another 40% or so were "O.K." The rest — over 50% — were absolutely terrible!

Fellow salespeople, you have a serious problem. One that should be solved immediately. You are trying to haul water and the bottom of your bucket is gone.

The Good Refrigerator
Is Only 18¢ More!

There probably isn't a single reader of this book in the world who hasn't heard of J. Douglas Edwards' famous phrase, *"Reduce it to the ridiculous."* But, as powerful as this selling concept is, rarely is it used effectively out in the real sales world.

Audiences used to love to hear Doug give examples of this simple technique, but he went to his grave wondering why so few really used it, in spite of the fact that virtually all of the very top sales producers in the world use it routinely!

Whether you're an old hand who has forgotten, or a brand new salesperson who hasn't yet learned it, perhaps it's time for a brief refresher course:

The customer looks at your product and says, "It costs too much." Try responding with, "Of course it does, sir."

What happens? He was ready to fight, but you agreed with him! He has no one to fight. That's the last thing he expected!

Now say, "Tell me, sir, how much too much does it cost?" When he gives you the figure, say, "Fine, sir. Let me ask you this question. How long do you think you'll own this [your product]?" When he gives you the number of years, say "That would be how much a year, sir?" When he answers, say "That would be roughly how much a month, sir?" And then, "That would be how much a week, sir?"

Get the picture? And you can go down to days, hours, minutes, and even seconds with some products or services! And Doug Edwards would have loved to be in your position. You see, the bulk of his sales career was before the advent of the pocket calculator. He worked with rough figures.

Skipping financing costs for a second, just to give you the validity of this basic concept, understand the following:

The difference between the $20,000 car they really want and the $15,000 car they might settle for is only $2.74 a day over the five years they'll probably have the car. Just $2.74!

The whole family will enjoy the $200,000 home versus the $125,000 home if they'll just invest an extra $6.85 a day over the thirty years they said they plan to live there. Per family member, that's only $1.71 a day! "Surely, Mr. Prospect, just your wife's happiness and comfort is worth $1.71 a day! Just $1.71!"

You mow your lawn once a week? Then the $600 riding mower is only $1.73 more for each Saturday you *ride* around mowing your yard instead of pushing that $150 mower for the next five years. Just $1.73!

Refrigerators last twenty years or more. The difference between the cheapest one you can buy and the best one on the market is only about 18¢ a day. Just 18¢!

Any Master Closer can surely collect an extra 18¢ a day for the vastly improved benefits they give his/her customers, right?

When price is a problem, **reduce it to the ridiculous!**

TIPS

Here's a breakthrough concept for sales managers with lots of courage and/or lots of faith in humanity. Under the proper circumstances, this sales motivation tool can produce astounding sales production!

First, let's remind ourselves where the terms "TIP" and "TIPS" come from. TIP means *to insure promptness* and TIPS means *to insure prompt service* — virtually the same thing. And a TIP is given to a waiter, for instance, in exchange for good service. Americans, however, have never really understood the concept. Let's think it through.

If you are trying to insure that a waiter gives you prompt service, when would you give him his TIP? Well, in many parts of the world they do it properly. They give it in advance of the desired service. You see, sophisticated people don't take a chance on getting bad service — they insure they get good service by paying for it in advance.

Unsophisticated people give their TIPS after their meals are over, when it couldn't possibly have any effect on the service rendered.

Get it? O.K., let's plunge on.

So if you are a courageous sales manager, try this the next time you are trying to motivate your people to extra heights of sales production. Give them their rewards in advance of the contest or promotion.

Here's how a client of mine does it. He sits down with each salesperson and figures out what the next realistic level of sales production is for that person. Then, together, they figure out the dollar value to the company of that new extra production goal. Then, together, they decide on an appropriate reward for the proposed performance. Then my client hands them the reward — **in advance** of the mutually developed sales goal!

That's right! You get your VCR or briefcase or set of golf clubs NOW! Why would he do that? Because it's the quickest, easiest, most effective way to convey his absolute belief in the ability of each salesperson! And because it makes the sales objective a "done deal," with only the technicality of making the actual sales left over!

But what if they don't reach the sales target? Well, eventually they will . . . and there are no more rewards for an individual until he earns the one he already has received. But what if he never reaches the target and leaves the company? You're out a briefcase or whatever. Big deal!

Obviously, this technique should be used in some proportion to each individual salesperson's capability. I've met salespeople to whom I'd give a new Cadillac in advance. And I've met salespeople I wouldn't bet a cheap pen and pencil set on.

No one said it would be simple or easy — just effective!

So what does TIPS really stand for? To insure productive salespeople! And how can you do that? Reward them in advance and put the burden of extra production where it certainly belongs — on them!

Just Fly the Plane, Son!
Just Fly the Plane!

Here's a problem all but the highest level of salespeople suffer from — distraction!

By distraction, I mean this: Selling is often similar to walking across a snake-infested minefield. No sooner do you start to settle in than a "sales snake" rears its ugly head and strikes! No sooner do you get its head chopped off than a mine explodes right behind you . . . then another . . . then another . . . then another! It's no wonder so many salespeople fall by the wayside! It's not for the weak of heart!

John Hyde, "the voice" you hear on so many cassette programs, is a Master Closer by anyone's standards. But he told me even he sometimes likens selling to performing brain surgery in the rear car of a speeding roller coaster — standing up!

There's a lot going on simultaneously in most selling situations, much of it totally unknown to you, much of it out of your control. So it's a good time to remember the old adage, *"It's not important what happens to you. It's important how you REACT to what happens to you. "*

I was reminded of this while reading something written by Ron Mansfield. Seems he had started taking flying lessons. His instructor must have had the same manual mine had, because he taught him with the exact same questions my flight instructor used on me years ago. If you ever take flying lessons, here's how it goes:

You're walking across the tie-down area towards your plane. It's about the tenth lesson. Seemingly out of the blue, your instructor turns to you and asks, "What's the first thing you should do if you suddenly discover a rattlesnake in the cabin at 3,500 feet?" Well, most people blurt out something about not making any sudden movements. Or saying a prayer. Or radioing the tower for an ambulance.

And now that he's got you going, a good instructor will nod at whatever you said, then hit you with another "what if" emergency situation. You, being new to the game and pleased with the reaction you got to your first answer, will probably come up with another terribly inventive way to cheat death. He'll then nod and ask another one. You'll smile and respond. Then, usually in the middle of about your sixth or seventh clever answer, you'll hear the instructor begin to scream, "NO! Wrong! Now listen to me! Get this through your head . . . just fly the plane! JUST FLY THE PLANE!"

The mountainsides and fields of the world are littered with the bleached bones of pilots who allowed themselves to become distracted at precisely the wrong moment. As Mansfield reminded me, there have been many disastrous commercial jet crashes caused because entire flight crews became focused on minor problems such as a burned-out light bulb, while their planes went straight into the ground!

You can't fly a plane safely if you're down in the cargo hold looking for the source of that funny noise. And you can't sell with the top professionals if you get distracted by every "bump in the night" that occurs during the sales process.

See, the mountainsides and fields of the sales world are also littered with the bleached bones of former salespeople. Salespeople who allowed themselves to become distracted, frenzied, distressed, taken off center and, ultimately, totally out of control.

What's the solution? Mental toughness. Singleness of purpose. Mental toughness. Tunnel vision. Mental toughness. Sales skill. Mental toughness. Constant practice. Mental toughness.

I'm not going to cover the entire sales process for you here. That's what the rest of this material and just about all of the other things I've written and recorded are about. What this section is about is getting you to do what you've learned and/or are learning to do, *no matter what the circumstances!*

Virtually anyone can be taught to fly a plane. In many respects, it's easier and safer than driving a car, right up until something unexpected happens. That's when the training kicks in! That's when the top pilots (the living ones) are separated from the amateur pilots (the dead ones). It's the same in selling! Any idiot can learn a simple sales presentation and close a reasonable number of sales, as long as nothing unexpected happens. That's when the sales training kicks in! That's when the top salespeople (the ones still in the business) are separated from the amateur salespeople (the ones who dropped out)!

It has been said of flying that it's hours of boredom interrupted by moments of stark terror! Selling is very similar. Although I've never found it boring, it can certainly become routine. And then, just when you're starting to relax, *stark selling terror!* A "sales snake" right under your seat! The cabin fills with "objection smoke." The "bulbs of reason" all burn out simultaneously! The "closing gears" refuse to go down! It is now, at this very moment, that we discover what we are made of. We discover if we are going to hit the mountainside of sales failure, or fly over it to a smooth landing in the green field of sales success.

And what will make the difference? Just two things. The training and education you have *before* that moment comes. And, when it comes, whether or not you've got the mental toughness to remember it and use it — no matter what!

In the Air Force they have a saying, "Never run out of altitude and ideas simultaneously." How true! It's basically the same in selling.

So, when you're up against it . . . when you're down in the sales trenches fighting with short sticks . . . when there seems no way out . . . remember what my flight instructor yelled at me one warm sunny morning: **"JUST FLY THE PLANE, SON! JUST FLY THE PLANE!"**

What Do You Do
For a Living?

Elmer Wheeler said, among other things, "Find a need and fill it!" Zig Ziglar said something to the effect that you can get what you want if you help enough other people get what they want first. Fred Herman said, "People don't buy drills, they buy holes!" See a pattern here?

All of the sales greats I've ever known have reached several of the exact same conclusions or revelations sooner or later. And they all reached those discoveries before anyone considered them great. We've covered many of those sales revelations before, and we'll continue to hit on them as long as I'm involved in this wonderful business, but for now, in this section, let's look at just one of those blinding flashes that come to all Master Closers eventually. That one being an under-standing of what it is you do for a living . . . or should be doing.

If you've been to sales seminars, read sales books, or watched and/or listened to sales tapes, you know that everyone has a catchy way of saying basically the same thing. Of trying to describe what it is you are supposed to be doing with your customers.

The old-fashioned high-pressure con men would tell you it's your job to "grab the money before they know what hit 'em." The new touchy-feely sales types will tell you the job is to counsel them to death, or at least to sleep! And if there are ten thousand other so-called sales experts out there, there are at least ten thousand other opinions floating around. So how are you supposed to rise to the top with all of this conflicting infor-mation buzzing through your head?

Well, first understand there's probably at least some va-lidity in almost all the things you've heard — *some!* As a friend of mine used to say, "At the base of every lie there is usually a nub of truth. The nub that makes the lie believable." But I want to try to cut through all of the smoke and haze and clarify what it is you *should* be doing in every selling situation, without exception.

Now hang in there for a minute. What I'm about to say you'll think you've heard before. But maybe one more time, phrased a little differently, I can help drive it home. It's a simple lesson, but one very few truly understand.

You aren't really a salesperson after all! Your goal in life shouldn't be to become a "Master Closer," although that's what the others will probably call you when you really hit your stride. Forgive them. They just don't understand!

Here's what you are supposed to be doing: You are sup-posed to be a professional provider of solutions to problems. Now watch out! If you tune out now, you'll miss what all of the sales amateurs always overlook. Pay attention!

You are certainly there to solve the problems that already exist, are evident, and could be spotted by any fool representing your line of products or services. And, if you do just that, you'll always be able to eke out a living in sales, "eke" meaning *to get with great difficulty and minimum result.* But you want more than that or you wouldn't be investing in this sales training material. Right?

So you must go several steps further. You must also be a professional provider of solutions to problems that aren't so evident and easy to spot! Problems the customer was only dimly aware of. Problems that only become clear and demand solutions after you arrive on the scene. Problems that may have gone unnoticed and, therefore, unsolved for years had you not shown up, pointed them out, dramatized them, and provided the solution that makes everyone happy again. And if you do just that, you'll always be able to make a comfortable living in sales, "comfortable" meaning *affording or enjoying basic physical comforts and security.* But you want even more than that or you wouldn't be investing in this sales training material. Right?

Well then, you must go to the last and top step of being a professional provider of solutions to problems. You must develop the ability to *create* problems that didn't exist at all (until you arrived, created them, pointed them out, dramatized them, and then — and only then — provided the solutions to these new potential catastrophes in their lives).

Get it? A complete salesperson, whether they are called "sales pro," "Master Closer," or whatever, is able to spot the obvious problem and solve it. He or she is able to spot the not-so-obvious problem and solve it. And he or she is able to create problems that didn't exist before and solve them too!

What does each level of problem solving understanding bring you in the way of income? My years of observation would lead me to believe that it's something like this:

If you can only cure the easy-to-spot problems, you'll earn only about 30% of the money that could be made in your same industry, with your same products, with your same customers. Salespeople in this category are like the little scavenger fish that follow sharks and whales around, eating the scraps and droppings of the big guys. They may never starve, but they are always close to it.

If you can move yourself up to the category of salesperson who sees and solves the less obvious problems, you'll start making about 70% to 75% of what a real top salesperson could make if he or she worked your territory instead of you. Salespeople in this category are similar to journeymen fighters or run-of-the-mill ball players. They are necessary to make the system work, but they never reach their full personal potential. Like worker bees, they are good for the well-being of the hive, but they don't get much out of it for themselves.

But what if you become the type of salesperson who can perform at both the first two levels *and also* "create" problems to solve on top of that? Well then, the sales world is your oyster! You are then one of the legends the others can only whisper about in awe. You are then earning 100% of the rewards available in your industry!

Yeah, yeah! "But then how do I close these people?" you say. My friends, people who know they have a problem, people who feel that problem, people who are hurting physically, mentally, financially, personally and/or spiritually because of that problem, don't need to be "closed." They need to be led to THE SOLUTION! Remember? You are a professional provider of solutions to problems — no matter where the problems come from!

Here's some good news: Most people you try to sell to, assuming they have been reasonably well qualified, already have a known problem that you could solve or help solve. They know it and you know it. And most of the rest of your customers have an equal number of problems, even if they aren't aware of them until you get there. As for the rest, you must create a need or a want that didn't exist until you arrived. And when you do, they suddenly have a problem! See? An unfilled want or an unsatisfied desire is a problem! It's like an unscratched itch.

Take a dentist, for an example. She has three basic types of patients (customers):

1. She has those who break off a tooth over the weekend. They have a problem. They know it and she knows it. This does not require a Master Closer. It requires a professional provider of solutions to problems. In this example, a dentist.

2. Then she has those who come in for routine teeth cleaning, but *she* discovers three cavities! They have a problem. And, thanks to her, they suddenly know it and she knows it. This does not require a Master Closer. It requires a professional provider of solutions to problems. In this example, a dentist.

3. Last, she has those who came in for a routine teeth cleaning and had no cavities. No broken tooth and no cavities. No problem to solve. Wrong! There are lots of problems to solve, after they are created! How about a fluoride treatment to make sure those teeth remain cavity-free? And how about a special treatment to brighten the teeth, so they aren't "ashamed to smile"? And how about a synthetic bonding treatment to permanently close that "embarrassing gap" they've always been so self-conscious about?

See? After they are told that yellow teeth probably make them ashamed to smile, that the gap must be embarrassing, and that they just lucked out with no cavities this time (but probably won't be so lucky next time), the customer/patient has three distinct problems. Problems that need solving. Problems that, once solved, will make their lives much more enjoyable. Does this require a Master Closer? No! It requires a professional provider of solutions to problems. In this example, a dentist.

By the way, you would be stunned at the number of doctors, dentists, chiropractors, and lawyers who are buying sales training material and attending sales seminars to learn how to increase their incomes by creating new problems to solve!

So get this through your head once and for all! If you want to become known as a Master Closer, a top professional sales pro, a "Top Gun" in selling, you must become a professional provider of solutions to problems. And you must be able to solve the obvious problem, the not-so-obvious problem, and the nonexistent problem, equally well. And to solve the nonexistent problem you must understand that an unfilled want (something you can create out of thin air) or an unsatisfied desire (which you can also create out of thin air) are both actually problems waiting to be solved. Begging to be solved!

So a man selling timeshare property is selling solutions to bad vacations and family fights. And a woman selling sports cars is solving the problem of appearing to be a nerd. And the person selling investments is solving the problem of impending poverty.

I know it's old. I know I've mentioned it other places. But it's so good I'll try one more time: Don't sell drills, sell the holes they make! Solve the problem.

As my old friend and fellow sales pro, Joe Sugarman, once wrote: **"Each problem has hidden in it an opportunity so powerful that it literally dwarfs the problem. The greatest success stories were created by people who recognized a problem and turned it into an opportunity."**

And when you get really good at this, they'll say you are a MASTER CLOSER!

The Winner's Profile

I'm frequently asked if there are any common denominators I've noticed among successful salespeople — the Master Closers. The answer is: Certainly! As Jim Rohn is fond of saying, "Success leaves clues!"

Admittedly, my list changes from time to time, from meeting to meeting, and from mood to mood. But, over the years, I've developed a standardized list of characteristics that are a pretty good measuring stick for you to use to chart your sales progress, or lack of it.

When you are wondering how you stack up against the real sales pros, here's what most seem to share (in no particular order).

The top sales pros have an innate understanding of what makes people tick. What motivates them. What stimulates them. Not for a second do they forget that people do things for their own selfish reasons, not *our* selfish reasons! That people are always thinking, "What's in it for me?" Their sales presentations are always honed with that knowledge in mind . . . and the presentations are usually crisp, interesting, exciting, and easy to understand. When the pros ask for the order, there is no doubt in the customer's mind about what's in it for them. They know!

This next characteristic of top sales pros hitchhikes on the first: The pros I know and work with all know how to ask for what they want — whether it's an order, a payment, a commitment, or some other call to action. They know because they are experts in quickly matching their customer's wants, needs, and qualifications to the various products and services that fill those wants and needs. Put bluntly, they decide quickly, right up front, exactly what they want from each customer they meet. Exactly.

With few exceptions, the sales pros I respect most are extremely good at communicating. They are articulate and charming. People enjoy talking with them and, while talking, don't have to wonder what is being said. The sales pro's conversation is sprinkled with colorful analogies, interesting anecdotes, and other expressions that bring the conversations to life. Most people talk in black and white — the sales pro always talks in Technicolor!

Although it should go without saying, all the top pros I know are respected members of their communities. They are respected because, among other things, their honesty and integrity are above reproach. They are known for their credibility. They have worked hard to create that impression. They work even harder to maintain it. They are, in a word, *trustworthy,* and everyone knows it!

And my favorite sales pros are very tuned in to other people. They have a sixth sense about them. Almost a "sensitivity radar." Even the amateurs can parrot, "If you help others get what they want, you can get what you want." But it takes a sales pro to find out what they *really* want! See, it's not a cute slogan, it's a finely tuned skill. And it all starts with a sensitivity to other people's precise wants and needs.

Want more? The top pros I know all have the ability to maintain control. Pleasantly, politely, delicately — but in control! Amateurs can do this too, but only under ideal circumstances. The pros do it then, of course, but they also do it when the going gets tough! When they are up against it, so to speak. When the heat's on. When the resistance is high. When the competition is keen. You'd hardly notice it. You'll rarely catch them at it. But, through sheer mental power and force of personality, they are almost always in complete control of the selling situation.

The last major characteristic of the sales pro, the Master Closer, is a two-parter:

First, they all seem to know what they personally want. They know what they want from life, from business, from each individual encounter. As the Reverend Jessie Jackson is fond of saying, "Keep your eyes on the prize!" Well, the very top salespeople never take their collective eyes off of their individual prizes (goals). They are pleasantly and gently relentless in the pursuit of their objectives. They don't lose sight of their goal and, no matter what they appear to be doing at any given moment, they are moving toward that goal(s).

And, part two, they honestly believe they deserve the goals, objectives, and success for which they are striving. Be careful! This is a subtlety most people miss. The top pros: (a) understand what they want, and (b) work towards it constantly (and usually achieve it) because, (c) they believe they have the right to have what they want, desire, deserve, and earn.

165

Be sure to catch the main word in the last paragraph. Without that one single sparkplug, you'll never reach the very top rungs on the success ladder of selling. The most successful people I've ever known in selling, and I've known just about as many as anyone alive, all believe they have a *right* to succeed. A *right* to succeed in life. In selling. And in the specific sales presentation they are giving right now. Not an inkling. Not a feeling. Not a hope. Not a prayer. A RIGHT!

Eric Butterworth once wrote, "Nothing stops the man who desires to achieve. Every obstacle is simply a course to develop his achievement muscle. It's a strengthening of his powers of accomplishment." And William Jennings Bryan really hit it on the head when he said, "Destiny is not a matter of chance; it is a matter of choice. It is not something to be waited for; but rather something to be achieved."

Apples to Apples,
Oranges to Oranges!

One of the favorite tricks of customers the world over is to challenge prices. The old "I-can-get-it-cheaper-down-the-street" scam.

The reason this ploy is so popular among our prospects and customers is that it works so well! They seem to understand, at least at the subconscious level, that we salespeople handle price objections with less skill than just about any other single objection, with the possible exception of "I've got to think it over."

Why do we find price objections so devastating? Several reasons.

First, many salespeople sincerely fear that their prices are too high and that the entire concept of selling is, in and of itself, a distasteful and somewhat unethical occupation. They react to the sound of "Your price is too high" as does a rabbit to the sound of a sudden shotgun blast.

Second — and even more damaging to the wallets of salespeople everywhere — we tend to confuse *price* with *value*. Remember, they are two entirely different subjects!

If price was the deciding factor in most selling situations, we wouldn't even need salespeople! We'd just produce products, hang a price tag on them, and stand back. If the product didn't sell, we'd keep cutting the price until it began to move. For that you don't need salespeople, you need people with good handwriting! See, customers can *read* prices, but they need professional, high-paid salespeople to *explain* values.

Third, we allow customers to play the shell game with us, one wherein they can change the specific object we are discussing at will. For instance, "Your suit is $499? Why, I can get a suit that *looks* just like it for $199 right across the mall!" See, the object ball just changed!

How can we as professional salespeople control our customers more effectively without appearing to control them more effectively? It's all in your state of mind!

Let's take it from the top — starting with the title of this section, "Apples to Apples, Oranges to Oranges."

You must keep only apples on the table when you are discussing apples, apple quality, and apple values. The minute you see a round, rough-skinned, orange-colored citrus fruit slipped onto the bargaining table, you must stop the game! That's the beginning of the customer scam of comparing oranges to apples. That will drive you into a futile defense of why your apple is priced higher than their orange. That's a no-win situation for you!

Customers are entitled to discuss whatever they want, even when it is just plain silly. But YOU are entitled to control the items under discussion at any single moment.

An example: We are selling apples. Suddenly there is an orange on the table. Stop the game. Point out the orange. Explain that apples and oranges can't be compared. Offer to remove the orange and discuss only the apples, or remove all of the apples and begin discussing oranges. It's their choice. Either one. But not both!

You must keep the game simple, fun, and easy for all to understand — including you!

See, the Rolls Royce you are selling *does* cost more than the Cadillac they looked at this morning. Would that really surprise any rational human being? And a 700-foot oceanliner costs more than your Rolls Royce. And the Empire State Building costs more than all of those put together! Which raises the most relevant and poignant question of all: "So what?"

Jimmy Rucker and I were deep-sea fishing one day. Jimmy had what turned out to be a rather large fish hooked. It was jumping and running, running from side to side, going deep and coming back up. And there, sitting calmly in his chair was Rucker. Except for dipping the rod slightly and taking a few turns on the reel occasionally, it was like he was part of some other happening. The disparity between his personal center of calm and all of the thrashing and splashing taking place a few hundred feet behind the boat was unbelievable!

Rucker noticed me watching him and his fish, and said, "Benjamin, it's a lot like selling isn't it? It appears far more confusing than it really is. The fish doesn't know how it all comes out yet, but I do. And that calms me."

Well, you too can stay calm if you control the flow of the game — one subject at a time, and only with like objects in play at any one time. That one simple process will remove a

169

large percentage of the personal frustration involved in selling. But you must have the courage to control it. Politely, smoothly, calmly — but control it!

And now we come to the price itself:

First, understand we've already solved a great deal of the price problem by simply keeping irrelevant objects and subjects out of the game. Now we must determine the language we are going to use.

Here's all I mean by "language." The customer is usually not an expert in your industry or in your product line. At the starting gun, his kneejerk reaction is to say, "What does it cost?" That's an extremely stupid question, isn't it? Compared to what?

Since we all agree the customer always has at least one question in his or her mind — that being, "What's in it for me?" — don't you owe it to your customers to let them know exactly what's in it for them? Notice I said "owe" it. This isn't some cheap trick to get their money and cheat them. Remember, I assume you're selling a high-quality, competitively priced product for which your customer is qualified. If that's true, you have an obligation or a trust to make sure the customer clearly understands the value of your product before making a decision to buy or not to buy. If you do any less and they don't buy, you have literally cheated them!

So develop the mindset that you will always keep the conversation/sales presentation clear, clean, crisp, simple — and, therefore, easy to understand. And that, during the course of every sales presentation, you will insist (however gently) that your customer knows the value of your product before making any serious decisions. Not just the price — that's a feature. The value — which is a benefit!

Example: I've got a client who sells a basic item for under $50. The deluxe version is $250. But they have a special package wherein you get both of those and a whole lot more for about $350. The "whole lot more" package is really an astounding value, but many people who had originally intended to spend only $50 didn't even want to hear the details, because it was seven times what they had planned on investing. Percentage-wise, that's the same as intending to spend $10,000 on a used car and having the salesperson try to bump you to the $70,000 Super-Deluxe Fish-Tailed Snark!

How did we solve the problem? We changed the special package to a one-time, first-order-only special. "Take it now or never," basically. And then we developed a pleasant way of explaining it to people who had just said they weren't interested at all and didn't even want to hear about it.

Basically this was the script:

"I understand. I do, however, want to keep my job, so I'd really appreciate your help. Since this is a first-order-only special offer, I have to state *in writing* that you at least heard the offer before you say 'no.' See, the worst call we ever receive is from a customer who finds out about the contents of the special package *after* he has already wasted his first-order privilege. So please bear with me for just a couple of minutes. Now, here's what you'll receive in the . . ."

Our results indicated that almost every single person who heard that simple explanation at least listened to the rest of the presentation. And, as a result, just about everyone who could afford it — took it!

Pretty good, right? But we improved it! Here's how:

Rather than wait for the problem to develop (it always did!), we put the explanation closer to the front of the presentation. As soon as the subject of the basic widget in question came up, the salespeople responded, "Excellent choice! As you probably know, there are three ways to get the benefits of that particular product. And since the third option is deeply discounted for new customers only, and only on their first order, let me run through your options for you so you don't waste your first-order privilege. First, there's the basic widget and it . . ."

Even better! See, we recognized the problem (the objection), raised it first, plowed through it by promising excellent benefits yet unknown to him, and got to give our entire presentation almost every single time!

O.K., the message is plain. Compare only apples to apples. Only oranges to oranges. Only quality cars to other cars of equal quality. Only view lots to other view lots. Only hand-tailored clothing to other hand-tailored clothing. And, in whatever style and manner makes both you and your customer comfortable, make sure all of your customers hear *everything* that is to their advantage, whether they think they want to hear or not!

What do I do if the customer simply doesn't have time to do it properly? I schedule an appointment at a time when he will be able to listen. I refrain from giving my presentation under rushed circumstances. Result? Most people, seeing I'm that serious, agree to listen on the spot! Others schedule a better time. "But don't you totally lose some?" you ask. Are you sitting down? The answer is CERTAINLY!

But understand: One of the qualities I've noticed in almost every top sales professional I've ever known is the ability to "close the briefcase" and walk away. Always remember, you are a highly trained professional. You are not a beggar, a clown, or a court jester. You *always* sell from a position of strength! ***Always!***

But We Always
Buy From Joe

For a variety of reasons, prospective customers are frequently hesitant to change suppliers. One of the main reasons was contained in that sentence itself: "change"!

But there are also other reasons. Inertia, for one. Do you remember from school? "A body in motion tends to remain in motion until acted upon by an outside force. And, likewise, a body at rest tends to remain at rest until acted upon by an outside force."

Then there's loyalty. An admirable quality, to be sure. But a quality that will cost you dearly when that loyalty is to one of your direct competitors.

And, of course, there's always the old "feeling of obligation." And although obligation is easier to overcome than loyalty, it can still be a formidable challenge.

What's the worst one? That's easy! It's also the most common one: All four! That's right. All four!

Almost all of your prospects (who are currently buying your type of product from someone else) will resist any change at all — even when that change is obviously for the better. And they'll be hard to turn in a new direction because of inertia. And they'll feel a sense of loyalty and obligation, even to a supplier who isn't really serving their needs as well as you can! People are really fascinating!

Well, that's why selling is the highest paid profession on earth! Because you and I are skilled sales technicians, we already know how to overcome the fear of change, the power of inertia, and even misplaced loyalty and obligation. Right?

Well, just for reminders and review:

Never fight your prospective customers! Never make them feel worse than they already do about the traitorous deed they are contemplating. Empathize with them! Be like the good guy cop ("I understand why you killed your mother. I often thought about killing mine. Tell me, exactly why did you finally do it?"). Help them through the emotional turmoil . . . and understand one of the biggest fears they face. Know what it is? Think about it for a moment. Not one salesperson in a thousand ever thinks about it, not once in their entire sales career! Why? Because they haven't a single clue!

Ready?

Above and beyond the fear of change, the power of inertia, the force of loyalty and obligation. Above and beyond the appeal of your product, its features, benefits, and cost advantages. Past the obvious pleasure of dealing with you and your wonderful company, they have a dread even worse than tomorrow's dental appointment for root canal work. It's that bad!

What could be that bad? Meeting with their *now former* supplier/salesperson and telling him that they've taken their business elsewhere. That they've betrayed him. That they've done something behind his back. Don't ever forget it! People *hate* confrontations. Just like you fear actually asking for the order, and just like they fear saying "no" if you do (did you know that?), they hate the thought of telling the guy who is already calling on them that it's over. And they'll continue to pay too much and suffer bad service to avoid it!

I'll tell you how an associate of mine overcomes that problem in a moment, but first let's see how to even get up to that point.

The best two responses I've ever observed and used are the following. Both simply redirect the loyalty aspect back to where it should have been all along. To themselves!

They are:

1. **"I understand, respect, and even admire your feelings, loyalties, and obligations to your current supplier. You, however, have an even greater obligation to your own business and its shareholders. You have a moral obligation to operate this business as efficiently and profitably as is humanly possible. And, as we've agreed, by letting us serve you . . ."**

2. **"Your sense of obligation and loyalty is truly admirable and should be commended. It is, however, costing you, your business, and its shareholders a lot of money in order to finance that position. And, as we've agreed, by letting us serve you . . ."**

Get it? You've got to acknowledge the situation. Even praise the feelings that created it. But then point out the perfectly normal, healthy, selfish (not greedy) justifications for moving on to a better situation for everyone.

And what does my associate do to remove the last obstacle, fearing confrontation with the previous supplier?

He says, "I think one of the most difficult things about an improvement like this is informing the previous supplier. When I was a young man I was going to move my savings account to a new bank, but I didn't want to have to face anyone at the old bank. Much to my relief, I signed a form and the new bank did it all for me! With that in mind, and knowing that XYZ, Inc. is a professional organization and will respect your decision, I'll be willing to notify them if you'd prefer. Would that be of assistance to you?"

Now I'll spot you that takes some courage, but courage is a *major* ingredient in just about all of the most successful sales-people I've had the pleasure of knowing. Isn't that true?

So how's YOUR courage quotient today?

Do Real Sales Pros Have to Close?

As you have probably gathered by now, I'm big on making closing easier by doing everything else exceptionally well beforehand. In other words, if you and your product enjoy an excellent reputation, if the product is priced competitively, if the quality is there, if you treat your customers fairly, squarely, decently, and by the rules, if you watch ALL of the little things — then the close, while certainly vitally important, is among the easiest and most pleasant parts of the sales process.

I hammer this single point home over and over in every book I write, every tape I record, and every speech and seminar I give. And to the precise degree you understand, accept, and absorb that single point, you will ultimately rise or fall in the field of professional selling.

That said, let me share the results of a fascinating scientific report recently completed by one of the nation's most respected and influential study groups. Perhaps cold hard statistics will help drag you over the line and make you more of a believer.

The group worked with, studied, and interviewed 1,500 salespeople over a period of twenty-four months. They scientifically and psychologically tested them. They interviewed their customers — both in their presence and privately. Then they took their raw results and fed them into a computer which also contained the salespeople's commission earnings and gross sales figures.

They then divided the salespeople into two major categories. They asked what percentage of the time the bottom 25% of the salespeople spent working in each of the four major elements of the sales process. And they asked what percentage was spent in those same four categories by the top 25% of the salespeople. "Bottom 25%" and "top 25%" both, of course, referring to gross sales and net income.

For your reference, the four basic elements of the sales process are, basically speaking: (1) determining the needs of the customer, (2) working jointly on solutions to those problems, (3) the actual sales presentation, and (4) attempting to close the sale.

You'd better sit down — the results may well astound you!

It seems that the poor folks among us, the bottom 25% of all salespeople, spend only about 4% of their time trying to discover what their customers need or want! Then they spend only 9% of their time jointly seeking solutions to those problems with their customers. They spend 33% of their selling time giving their actual sales presentations, without knowing the customer's true problem or how to solve it! And, as you may have guessed, they spend the bulk of their time — an amazing 54% of their total sales effort — "trying to close." **54% of their time trying to close!** And, based on the way they spend the rest of their time, it would be valid to ask, "Trying to close what?" They couldn't possibly know what the customers were seeking!

And how do the rich folks among us (the top 25%) spend our selling time? I'll bet you've already got a good idea by now! Here it is:

The top 25% of the salespeople in the United States spend, on the average, a whopping 53% of their time determining the needs of their customers! 53%! And then they spend another 31% working with their customers to arrive *jointly* at solutions to those problems!

Take note: Steps 1 and 2 take up 84% of their total time, and they haven't even begun their sales presentations! Is it getting clearer to you yet?

And the winners among us then spend just 11% of our total selling time giving our "official sales presentation"! Now get ready . . . the top 25% spend only 5% of their time "trying to close" their sales! *Just 5%!* And these salespeople make 80% of all the sales commission dollars earned! 80%!

You can fight my personal opinion all you wish . . . and I don't blame you, because I fought it too, for years! But, if there is a small group of people earning 80% of all sales commissions available, and if that small group spends 95% of their time doing something other than closing, you ought to find out what it is they're doing! And you'd better get good at it quickly!

What about the 50% in the middle? Well, these are the average salespeople, floating somewhere between the top and the bottom, suspended by the sheer force of our general economy. The people who are the best of the worst and worst of the best. It seems they tend to spend their time equally divided between the four areas of selling — almost exactly 25%, 25%, 25% and 25%.

When asked why, they said they didn't really know. And that's the point! They *didn't* know! They *don't* know! They'll *never* know! They haven't a clue! They are just run-of-the-mill average folks, the little grey people of selling. The worker bees.

Here's the good news. You don't have to be one of them anymore! You now KNOW better!

You might as well give in. I'm not going to give up on this point, I assure you! Remember, there is no right way to do something wrong!

Your Price Is Outrageous!

Have you ever had a prospect say that to you? Well, as Paul Newman said in the movie, *Cool Hand Luke,* "What we have here is a failure to communicate."

And, whether your customers or prospects have said it to you or not, I'll bet many have at least thought it — and that killed your sale. Unless, of course, you were astute enough to recognize it, ferret it out, overcome it, and close the sale anyway.

O.K., let's take the basic objection we frequently hear in one form or another: "Your price is too high."

What does that really mean? Well, if you're selling overpriced products, it might just mean your price IS too high! If that's the case, you'd better do something quickly or begin selling your family on the values of a low-calorie diet program.

If, however, your price is at least reasonable and competitive, "your price is too high" means something else entirely. It means you have not yet raised the perceived value of your product to the point where it exceeds the dollar amount you are requesting in exchange. You see, the truth is that when the perceived value of your product meets or exceeds the price you are asking, a *qualified* customer will take it every time — unless they don't have the money at that particular moment. And if they don't have the money, that's not a price objection anyway. It's a financial condition unique to them.

Here's a personal example. There is an item I sell for which I charge about $150. Except for the time involved, it is virtually pure profit. So when I look at your widget, I automatically convert the price of it into the number of my widgets that I have to sell in order to pay you for yours. For instance, I can sell my $150 widget in a few minutes while sitting at my desk in my cozy, comfortable office. So when you offer to sell me a load of firewood that you had to go buy, cut down, cut in lengths, split, load, deliver, and stack behind my house for $150 — I'm in! That's value!

In fact — and I want this kept just between you and me — I'd pay a great deal more for firewood than I do if I had to. A great deal more!

So always make sure you have the perceived value as high as possible for each individual customer *before* you go asking for a cash exchange. If you'll do just that, you'll get far less price objections.

Here's another price objection: The "price of change." People hate change of almost any kind. Among other things, they hate changing suppliers — especially if it means having to learn something new, or unlearn something old. In these situations, especially if the savings or benefits are marginal, you must overcome the price-of-change objection by not only raising the perceived value of your product, but by guaranteeing to make the change as painless as is humanly possible.

And what do you do about the price ticket shopper? Simple! Do all of the things we've already discussed, plus add the element of urgency (i.e., "This price is guaranteed through this Friday at 5:00 PM PST. After that, all prices are subject to change."). Don't forget that people act out of hope of reward or *fear of loss!*

Understand that "price" is a term customers often use, but "value" is the term you should use.

Here's an example of value. Some people ordering *The Closers* over the years have expressed surprise at the retail price we charge for a paperback book, so we've trained our salespeople to point out that we aren't selling paper weight, or covers, or pretty pictures. We are selling **information.** Information that could double, triple, or quadruple their incomes. Now, let's say you are making $30,000 a year and I've got a book containing information that can turn that into $75,000 per year. What's the book's *value?* $45,000! And when $45,000 in value is compared to the $24.95 price, is *The Closers* overpriced? Of course not! It's a steal! In fact, it would be a steal at $45,000 if I had the only copy in existence! Right?

There are two ways that I could conclude this section. One is to tell you that, because of what we've just covered, no legitimate product or service is ever overpriced — some are just undervalued by their own salespeople. But I think it might be a clearer lesson if I put it this way: ALL products and all services are, without exception, OVERPRICED — unless, and until, professional salespeople attach proper value to them.

The legendary late, great sales trainer, Fred Herman, was trying to explain this concept to me one day. As I'm sometimes a little slow on the uptake, he was getting frustrated. Then he said, "Ben, I would like to track down the mutual fund sales-man that called on me in 1960 and beat him within an inch of his life!" To which I replied, "Why? Did he oversell you?" To which Fred replied, "NO! He didn't sell me anything! He wasn't good enough to build the value of dollar cost averaging investing in my mind, so I didn't start buying! I figure he cost me about a half million dollars in profit so far!"

You see? It really isn't the actual price anyway! It is the **perceived value** and that is something YOU can control!

Remember what Robert Collier said about perceptions: "The source and center of all man's creative power . . . is his power of making images, or the power of imagination."

One In the Hand
Is Better?

The old adage, "A bird in the hand is worth two in the bush," is certainly true. But, if you are a good salesperson, you want the one in your hand *and* the two in the bush! Right?

We were talking about that dilemma the other day in a sales training seminar I was conducting. The problem was raised by a salesperson with a selling situation you've probably encountered in some form or other.

His basic widget sells for about $300, but they have a far better package containing almost $2,000 worth of widgets for about $1,000. His company only uses the better package as an introductory special and as an "upsale" and he's only allowed to mention it *after* the customer has agreed to take at least the basic $300 widget.

It's a very good selling situation most of the time because the *value* of the better package far exceeds the asking price. The problem comes when a customer wants the better package but hesitates because of the additional outlay of $700. And that hesitation was often turning into lost sales — including the original sale of the basic widget!

It seems that many customers who couldn't afford the better deal wanted to "think it over" and, in the process, became bitter because of what they were losing by not being able to take the better deal. So they ordered *nothing!*

So why didn't he just resell them on the smaller package that they had already said they wanted? Well, he did with some of them, but it took at least two calls to do it and he was still missing quite a few.

Why was this happening? Simple! Because he was letting go of the first sale entirely when he went for the up!

Here's how we solved it for him:

His new approach is to completely wrap up the first lower sale. And I mean signed, sealed, and all but delivered. Then, and only then, he covers the more expensive special — saying that it is a special reward made available only to the people who actually bought the original basic widget, as a way of saying "Thank you!"

Surprise! Many people began taking the special package not as an up, but as an *addition* to the original sale! And, of course, a few still said they just couldn't afford it. Remember: that is a condition, not an objection!

But what about the "think-it-over" people he was completely losing before? Well, don't forget, he now has a firm, signed order in his briefcase. So, after trying all of the normal "I-want-to-think-it-over" reverse techniques, he simply puts it back on them. He says, "Well, I certainly understand. How much time will you need to think it over?" Then, no matter what length of time they say, he says, "Good! I'll wait until then. And if you don't elect to take the special package, we'll ship the order you placed today the very next morning. But either way, I want you to know I really appreciate your business and look forward to working with you. Have a super day!"

Results? He says he hardly ever leaves empty-handed now. He usually gets the up. Sometimes he gets it as an addition. And, at the worst, he has the one he had to begin with!

So don't forget, one in the hand is *not* always better than two in the bush! The two in the bush are *better* than the one in the hand IF you learn how to control the bush! And, better yet, keep the one in the hand, get the two in the bush, and look for some more bushes!

Control your selling situation! And remember what Marden said: "The golden opportunity you are seeking is in yourself. It is not in your environment; it is not in luck or chance, or the help of others; it is in yourself alone."

Ask Them!
They Are the Experts!

I t never ceases to amaze me how many times otherwise good solid salespeople miss taking advantage of their best possible source of information. Information that can spell the difference between hits or misses in selling.

Who are these untapped sources of knowledge and wisdom? The very people you are trying to sell. Your customers!

Understand this: You may not know why she didn't buy. It may be a total mystery to you. You may not have a clue. But it's no mystery to *her!* She knows exactly why she didn't buy! And if you ask her in a polite, non-threatening manner, she will probably tell you! Then, at the worst, you'll have at least learned something from the experience. And at the best, you'll have a fresh opportunity to solve the problem, overcome the objection, meet her needs, and make the sale. Isn't that worth a shot?

You know what most salespeople do? They leave the only person who could possibly know why she didn't buy, then drive to their sales manager's office and ask him. How would he know? He wasn't there! He hasn't got a clue!

I've got a friend, the national sales manager of an after-market auto supply company, who has at least one solution. If you work for him, you'll probably try that stunt only once in your entire sales career.

Here's what he does:

The new salesperson walks into my friend's office (the old ones have already learned the hard way), his tail is between his legs, and he tells his tale of woe. My friend listens intently. Then, at the end of the story, my friend says, "Well, *exactly* why didn't she buy?" The young salesperson confesses that he doesn't know and didn't ask. So my friend picks up the phone, calls the prospective buyer, and asks the question the salesperson should have asked point blank.

It usually goes something like this: "Barbara, this is Jim. I've got a favor to ask of you. Have you got a minute? [pause] Good! Stan, my new salesperson, called on you earlier today and didn't get the order he had hoped you would place. Barbara, I've got high hopes for Stan, but he isn't going to make it in selling if he doesn't get better real quick. He's here in my office now and I'm going to put you on the speaker phone so you can tell him *exactly* why you didn't order today — seems he forgot to ask you while he was there with you! [pause] O.K. Barbara, go ahead. Exactly why didn't you order today? And I want you to be totally honest, so Stan can serve you better in the future."

Does that send a chill up your spine? How would you like to experience that session, first-hand? Well, if you did, I bet you'd ask lots of questions the next time a prospect turned you down . . . or hesitated . . . or anything else!

So what do you ask? What is this "questioning technique" most of the top sales pros use so effectively?

First, let's make sure our thinking process is in order. Questioning is an honest, effective, totally legitimate method for serving our customers better. Remember, you are not some sleazeball trying to cheat your customer out of her life savings. You are a sales professional, offering high-quality products at competitive prices to qualified buyers who have a legitimate need or want for your type of product. Got the picture?

O.K., with that in mind, let's put on our doctor/salesperson attitude hat.

Picture this: You're in your doctor's office. You called for an appointment because you've been having intense pain in your kidney area, coupled with a discharge from your left ear. The doctor comes in, shakes your hand and says, "What seems to be the problem?" You say, "I have this pain down here and . . ." wherein the doctor interrupts and says, "Here, take these green pills and call me in thirty days. Thanks for coming in." The doctor then walks out of the examination room.

Quick, tell me! How did that feel?

What's the problem? Did you feel the doctor should have determined the problem before he prescribed the medicine? Did you feel that perhaps the green pills may not be the perfect solution for everyone? Well, that's *exactly* how your customers feel when you barge through your presentation, ignoring their sincere questions and concerns!

And, when they say "no," frequently they are just expressing their frustration about your "Here, take these green pills" approach.

So when should you ask questions? Here's when: Too soon. Too often. Repeatedly. Constantly. And of course, always.

In other words, not just when you are morbidly curious about why you just lost the last sale, but as part of your overall sales and selling system!

You may phrase it a thousand different ways, but here's the "blanket question" to which you are trying to get an answer: "Why do you feel that way?"

See, a price objection can mean many different things. The three most common ones are: (1) you haven't yet built the perceived value to match the price, (2) the price is too high (versus the competition), and (3) he doesn't have the money to buy.

So before you go solving the price objection, you must question your customer to discover *which* price objection we are dealing with. The examples I've just used are three separate and distinct problems. Green pills might solve one of them, they can't solve the other two. Not a chance!

The objection may be based on fact, rumor, or misinformation. If you discover the exact objection and the reasons behind it, you should be able to put it to rest. For instance, your customer may have heard your product has a quality or service problem — when in fact, *Consumer Reports* says yours is the most trouble-free widget in the world! Only direct questioning will root out this piece of misinformation, thereby enabling you to clear the air and make the sale.

Now here's the **questioning technique secret** that all the top sales pros I know use: They don't rely on quick thinking and fancy footwork to save them at the last moment. As we've discussed elsewhere in this book, your product or service has certain standard objections built into it. You hear the same ones over and over — with a few rare surprises thrown in just to make things interesting. So you don't wait for your customer to hit you with one of the golden oldies before you dream up an appropriate fact-finding question. Do your work in advance!

How? Write down all of the objections you ever hear about your widget. All of them! Put each one at the top of a single sheet of paper. Then fill out the rest of each page with the questions you would use to follow-up on each conceivable objection. Then memorize them and drill yourself until it becomes automatic to respond with the proper question or series of questions.

Understand, the real pros in the sales industry aren't necessarily the quickest thinkers, but they are the best prepared!

Just like a top professional boxer, your reactions to most selling situations should have been programmed into your brain long before the actual sales event. If you have to stop and dream up each reaction from scratch, they'll soon count you out of selling — just like a poor, untrained, amateur boxer.

Remember, the harder you work, the luckier you get!

The Knife Man

It finally happened! We've all kidded about the salesperson who won't let the customer buy until he finishes the sales presentation. I don't mean the salesperson who just isn't paying attention and misses buying signals, I mean the legendary, mythical salesperson who *refuses* to let you have the product until he goes through his entire presentation. Don't think he exists? You're wrong! We met him at the California State Fair!

I love live product demonstrations. *Love 'em!* And I've got a home full of gadgets to prove it. So I take John Hyde, famous sales trainer and narrator of *The Closers* new cassette program, along with me to the fair. Then I drag him to my favorite area to watch the salespeople do their magic.

The first demo table we see has the world-famous knives you see on TV. I have a set (make that several sets!) and I'm wild about them. So I told John he should pick up a set for himself. He agreed and we walked up to the table where we were the only ones there.

The demonstrator looked up and I said, "Here's a lay-down sale for you. My friend here has seen my set and wants one of his own. How much does he owe you?"

Are you ready for this? He says, "I'll start the demonstration as soon as I have five other people." To which I replied, "He doesn't need the demonstration, he just wants to buy a set. How much does he owe you?"

Did you think he just misunderstood me? Wrong! He replied, "Unless I demonstrate it properly he won't know how to use it." So I said, "John is almost 50 years old. Trust me, he knows how to use a knife. How much does he owe you for a set?"

Picture this: John is standing there with his wallet open and there is a $100 bill clearly in view.

The man's reply? I *swear* this is true! He says, "Put yourself in my shoes. If I just sell him a set, I'll only sell one set. But if I wait until there is a crowd, then demonstrate the set, then he buys, I'll sell several more. So you guys will just have to wait for the demonstration."

Well, by this time John and I were laughing so hard we had to hang on to the man's demonstration table to keep from falling down. Finally we pulled ourselves together and, continuing on down the aisle, we quickly came upon another man selling the same knife with even better "extras" in the set. I told him the same thing I had told the first man.

His response? He *instantly* handed John a bag bulging with knives, juicers, and other bonus items and said, "That'll be just $24.95 plus tax. $26.45 total. And thank you very much! By the way, if you'd like to see the full demonstration, you're welcome to stay. You'll get more use out of these if you know how best to use them."

Did we stay for the demonstration? You bet! Did we learn new ways to use the knives? You bet! Are we happy customers? You bet! And was the second man a closer? You bet! How many did he sell when he did his full demonstration? He went nine for nine! With us, it was ten for ten!

Folks, let them have your product when they ask for it! And if you've still got another extra sales presentation bottled up inside of you, save it for your dog when you get home. He *needs* your attention!

Gigi's Plan A and Plan B Interview

One of the dearest, sweetest people I've ever known also happens to be a real estate agent. Her name is Gigi and, when you work with her, you have complete confidence in her ability, her integrity, and her concern for your welfare. She personifies the message in *The Closers:* "Sum Tertius" (My God first. The other fellow second. I am third.) I'm proud to call her a good friend.

That's the personal side. Now let me share with you the professional side. In particular, what I call *Gigi's Plan A and Plan B Interview.*

Seems Gigi quickly tired of being a real estate tour guide for every morbidly curious couple who fell through her office's front door. She especially tired of wasting her floor time and her "ups" on people who were totally unqualified to buy, or who were just double-checking on some other agent, or who wanted her to do the legwork for them (before they actually bought from their old Uncle Harry, a part-time agent across town).

Asking Gigi to become tougher, more aggressive, or highly assertive would be like asking the Pope to become a professional mud wrestler, so she decided to take another approach to the problem.

First, she decided to begin qualifying her prospects much more thoroughly right up front. No more driving people around looking at other people's high-priced homes when the prospects didn't have enough gas to get back to their own rented apartment! But how does a nice, well-mannered, gentle lady do that without becoming offensive? Easily! She developed a detailed, but non-threatening, personal and financial questionnaire. And she created a simple little script to precede it.

Oversimplified, the script goes something like this:

> *Please come into my office and sit down for a moment. I'm very sensitive to your time considerations, so I'd like to get a clearer understanding of exactly what you have in mind. That way I can be of maximum assistance to you."*

Simple enough? And she says that as she walks to her desk, never looking back or waiting for their approval.

Now for the questionnaire: She gathered up all of the financial and personal questionnaires she could find in her office, at the stationery store, at the local banks, and from the trade associations she belongs to. From them she pulled the most important qualifiers that would ultimately determine what, if anything, a prospect would and could buy. Then, to go *in front* of those financial questions, she created a series of lifestyle questions (i.e., How many bedrooms? What do you want most in a new home? And least?, etc., etc.). Then she put all of the questions into conversational phrasing form, so they sounded casual and relaxed. Then she typed it up in a simple checklist format.

Now, as they all sit down at her desk, she says,

> *"I've developed a little checklist to help me help you. It's nothing official, just notes to guide me to exactly what you really want. Let's see, your first name is spelled _____? And your last name is _____? And your daytime phone number is _____?"*

And away she goes. Then, when she has everything the form calls for, she's ready to reveal Gigi's Plan A and Plan B. She says,

> *"Now, oversimplified, there are two basic ways I can work with you. If you'd prefer to just wander around the area on your own, I'll be happy to give you some addresses of homes that seem to fit the general profile we've designed here today. You can then call me when you see something that interests you and I'll arrange to meet you for a tour of the home. Some people prefer this arrangement because there is absolutely no obligation on your part to buy through me unless you stumble across something you really like on my list. And, because I'll have little or no time invested, I won't be offended if you ultimately do business with someone else on a house they told you about.*
>
> *"The other way of working together is designed for those who are really serious about finding the home they want, and for those who can see the advantage of drawing on my experience and knowledge in this particular market. For people who want to work with me*

this way, I literally become your partner. I'll take you wherever and whenever you want to go. I'll find new listings for you to tour. I'll help with your financing. With your moving. I won't rest until you are comfortably settled in your new home . . . and even then I'll check with you a couple of times a year just to touch bases.

"Under this second option, my Executive Plan, I promise a full-scale commitment to you and, in return, I merely ask that you return the commitment by making me your exclusive real estate representative for the purpose of locating your home in this area. Fair enough?"

If they say "yes" at that point, they agreed to Plan B, or they may ask a few more questions before deciding. Either way, at least you both know where you stand and under what basis you will go forward.

Whichever plan they choose, she hands them a simple form that has both options on it. Described in simple layman's language, it is merely a gentleman's agreement. They check the box next to the plan they picked and sign it. She gives them the original and keeps a copy. Simple enough?

Gigi tells me she's never tried to enforce one of these informal agreements, but that the problem has only come up once or twice anyway. She says the psychological commitment seems stronger than any legal commitment!

Helpful hint: If you want to try this type of approach, let the questionnaire, your script, and the final agreement form do the dirty work for you. Remove yourself from the process psychologically. You are, for these few first moments, like a government clerk filling out one of their standard forms. Don't even look up! The attitude is, "The form is asking you these personal questions, not me."

Where can this approach and/or attitude work? In just about any selling situation where it's likely to take awhile to consummate the sale. That would include most, if not all, big-ticket items. And it's highly effective for anyone who has been clever enough to establish themselves as an unbiased expert in their chosen field. I've seen it used effectively with just about all but very few low-ticket items and in one-call selling — where you only have one shot at writing an order. Everywhere else, it's a powerful tool!

So why doesn't everyone use it? Because it takes courage to risk the entire sale right up front, and courage is always in short supply! As the Spanish say, "It is courage that vanquishes in war, even more than good weapons."

Saving the
Ruined Sale

Whether you personally did it, the outside delivery service did it, one of your own support departments did it, it was an "act of God," or it was done by the Gremlins who seem to inhabit the sales world, a sale that gets ruined and is not quickly saved by a sales professional is among the most costly events in selling. Even more costly than not having made the sale in the beginning!

Remember, unlike a sale that was never made, you now have hard costs involved (travel, entertainment, time, order processing, shipping, production, etc.) and, if you're like many salespeople, the commission may have already been spent! (I've found it was always easier to budget and allow for the thousand dollars I never made than it was to give back the thousand dollars I'd already received. Agreed?)

O.K., if we understand that we must deal with these situations quickly and efficiently, here's how you do it:

First, don't forget all of the skills, charm, and professionalism you originally used to get the order in the first place! **This is still selling.** In fact, one could argue it's selling in one of its higher forms. So don't forget the basics and don't try to become something you're not. You screwed up. That's too bad. But it's not the end of the world and it's not time to grovel around on the floor with your tail between your legs.

Next, take action *quickly.* Remember how enthused you were when you first got the order? How quickly you jumped on anything your customer needed? Well, *triple* that speed and *quadruple* that enthusiasm! As someone once said, "The best defense is a good offensive."

Ideally, you'll find out about the goof *before* your customer discovers it. If you're lucky enough to be in that position, don't let the advantage get away from you! Whether by phone, fax, mailgram or personal unannounced visit, be the one to break the bad news. It'll take most of the sting out of the situation — just like when your young child tearfully tells you she accidentally broke your favorite vase (versus you first finding it hidden under the sofa!).

Fast action and visibly displayed concern will cure a world of hurts — if it's right up front! See, all a customer really wants to believe is that you have their best interest at heart. Remember "Sum Tertius"?

Next, utter one of the two hardest phrases in the entire language. Say, **"I'm sorry."** (The other difficult one is "I don't know.") And don't try to soften your role in the matter by saying "We're sorry," or "The company is sorry," or "The Shipping Department said to say they are sorry." Say you are sorry . . .

and take full responsibility for the error, whether it was your fault or not. Your customer will appreciate you *and* this change of pace, since the last ten salespeople all blamed *their* mistakes on someone else!

Make sure your customer knows you are hurting as much as he is. Show your empathy (you know how he feels). And show your embarrassment. If you do it properly, they'll feel so badly for you they'll wind up apologizing to you!

Next, purge yourself. You must atone for your sins! You must do some form of penance. You must pay a penalty. You must give him some satisfaction! Depending on the importance of your blunder, the size of the order, and your relationship with the customer, this "penance" could take many forms. It might mean giving a special discount (my least favorite, because it could tend to lessen the true value and price of your product or service in his eyes). Or waiving shipping costs (better). Or extending his warranty (excellent, if you have a good product!). Or maybe just taking him out to lunch or to your country club for a round of golf. Whatever. But make sure he has something that *proves* you really did care!

Then confirm and follow up. You want to make sure he really has become satisfied again. This serves the same function as "post-selling" served at the conclusion of the original sale — but it's even more important now! Understand, if you drop the ball now, you'll never get it back.

But what's this all got to do with closing, you say? Well, first of all, it IS closing! You are closing a sale you messed up — and that's FAR more difficult than it was to close it the first time. And second, if you do it exactly as I've suggested, you've just closed the *next* sale — and you haven't even given the presentation yet!

It would probably be far more exciting to go in cold next time. To outwit him. To dazzle him with all the new closes you've learned. But, speaking just for me, I'll take the easy, lay-down, pre-closed sale from a grateful and trusting customer every single time! How about you?

All customers, all employers — the entire business world is constantly seeking salespeople who can and will do the difficult and the unusual. Salespeople who think and who take action. Salespeople who attract success by constantly performing more than is expected of them. Become one of those special salespeople!

Getting Them To Buy Your Offer

Whether you have a workable, successful sales presentation now, or are still trying to develop one, it's important you understand the elements that go into all successful presentations. With that information, you'll know why your presentation works or why it doesn't, and how to improve it in either case. In other words, it's no longer enough to have just a workable sales pitch because, should something change (your job, your product, your industry, your pricing, the economy, etc.), you'd have no way of building a new presentation that would fit your changed situation.

Don't leave it to chance that your customers will arrive at proper conclusions as a result of merely hearing and seeing your presentation. Odds are they won't! And customer surveys repeatedly show that customers *want* you to tell them specifically what it is they're supposed to have understood! It's a fact that you'll sway more customers, change more opinions, and get more sales if you'll draw firm conclusions for your customers at the end of all of your sales presentations.

Next, understand that there are always at least two sides to any agreement, and at least two conclusions that can be drawn from any statement — or *sales presentation.* That's an indisputable fact. What's not so clear, however, is knowing when you should ignore this fact of life, versus when you need to deal with it as an integral part of your sales presentation. Here's the answer: You have the luxury of dealing with just one side of the issue *only* when your customer already agrees with you, has said so, and realistically won't be coming in contact with the other side of the story anyway. Or when you are regarded as the ultimate authority in your industry and as regards your product or service. Failing those conditions, you must personally present the other side within the framework of your own sales presentation. Especially when you have reason to believe that your customer knows a good deal about your product and/or other products like it. Or when your customer was strongly opposed to the idea in the beginning — *no matter what he says now!* Or when you know or believe he's going to be exposed to the other side in the near future anyway. If there is going to be some bad news for your side, best you present it in the most favorable light. Don't leave this vital task to some "friendly competition." There's no such thing!

Next, whenever possible, try to gain what basketball players call the "home court advantage." Admittedly, this isn't possible in all selling situations. But when it is, use it to your advantage! All else being equal, you'll sell far more when sitting in your office or home, or even in a restaurant where you are well known, than you will on their home turf. There is a psychological advantage to being in charge of the physical as well as the mental stage!

Next, as all salespeople have been told time and time again, people buy out of **"hope of reward"** or **"fear of loss."** Usually a little of both. So make sure your sales presentation hits those two motivators *solidly*. However, that's just not enough! Your sales presentations must also acknowledge and deal with four other emotional motivators and, to the degree you do, your income will soar! They are: **Trust** (or faith) **and assurance** (or security). **Rewards** (prizes, awards, or accolades) **and recognition**. **Independence** (freedom, autonomy, or wealth) **and strength** (power, omnipotence, or energy). And last, but not least, improvement in their physical position, their job, their income, their social position, and/or **their own personal status**. Hit all or most of those points in your sales presentations and you'll be astounded at how easy selling becomes!

And then make sure your sales presentations contain plenty of emotion (the real reason people buy) and just the right amount of logic (the real reason people buy). See a contradiction there? Well, you shouldn't! People need emotion and logic in order to buy. It isn't one or the other. It's a question of the proper "mix" — just as any good recipe always has more than one ingredient. So, while it's true that emotion is the *dominant* factor in most buying decisions, it's also true that you must provide the proper amount of "sales yeast" to make it all rise . . . and sales yeast is the **logic** that allows them to justify and explain their buying decisions to themselves and to others (bosses, friends, spouses, etc.).

Next, it's important that you state the points backing your claims and positions in a clear and specific manner. You'll always gain more ground and make more sales dealing in positive specifics than you will with generalized "fuzzies." And generously lace your sales presentations with analogies, actual examples, and case histories. People are bored and distracted by most statistical information — unless it is responding to a specific question *they* asked (so have it ready, just in case!).

Next, although perhaps not as a set part of your planned presentation, constantly look for opportunities to have your customers perform small favors for you. Why? Psychological study after psychological study at major universities and think tanks all over the world keep uncovering this interesting phenomenon: If a person can be persuaded to do a favor for you, no matter how small or insignificant or frivolous, they are *far more* likely to perform another and larger favor for you. And another. And another. Perhaps even to the point of **buying something** they were otherwise inclined not to buy. Strange but true!

Then make sure your sales presentation has a "step down" built into it. I know people who always appear to be trying to sell a much larger package than they actually intend to sell — or ever have sold, for that matter. Charities are wonderful at using this technique! See if this sounds familiar: "Would you be able to contribute $100 to our fund drive?" Then, when the target declines, they say, "Then how about just $20?" which was all they expected to get to start with! But guess what. That approach also garners many extra $100 checks as a bonus!

After you hit them with the higher figure (or suggested order) and they decline, simply say, "Then how many do you want?" or "Then how much do you want to give?" See? You ignore the "no," assuming it was just a matter of quantity.

And last, check your presentation to make sure it has a "fall-back" position built into it as an optional approach. This might be as simple as providing a test period, or trial offer, or an exceptionally strong satisfaction guarantee. I don't want you selling from a position of weakness, but there are times when they simply won't buy if they can't try it out for a period of time. Be ready for it and be prepared to cash in!

I repeat: Whether you have a good sales presentation now
. . . are trying to revamp one . . . or are putting together your
first one . . . make sure it contains all of these elements, or as
many as can conceivably match your product or service within
the constraints of reality. That's **"reality,"** not weakness!

As you slowly build your own personal and powerful
sales presentation, you will experience disappointments, I
promise you. But keep at it! Remember that Edison tried
hundreds of times to create the light bulb. And, near the end —
but before he discovered the right filament — he said, "I have
not failed. I have successfully discovered 1,200 materials that
won't work."

Well, it won't take you 1,200 attempts, I promise you
that. But I also promise you the first one won't be right either.
Keep at it!

★ ★ ★

And
Another Thing ...

As I mentioned before, one of the by-products of almost thirty years of aggressively studying successful salespeople and what makes this whole thing called "selling" work is a huge stash of powerful sales material. I've got thousands of loose notes, notebooks, tapes, books, audio tapes, videotapes, and more than my share of matchbook covers and cocktail napkins — all crammed with fascinating sales material.

A lot of what I have is standard issue sales stuff, available to anyone bright enough to buy it and study it. But the best information usually comes in unofficial form, like in a nice restaurant after the sales day is over. That's when the war stories are heard from the best in the business. And it's why I've got thousands of bits and pieces of ideas bubbling up out of file drawers and storage boxes all over the office.

Many of these are just snatches of good ideas, not long enough to devote entire sections to. So I'm now going to unload a few shoeboxes on you, in no particular order. Use them when and if you wish. They are gifts to you from some of the very top sales pros from all over the world.

Have Faith in Quality

This is one that pops up in dozens of notes I've taken. My personal experience has proven it true time after time. Contrary to what you hear constantly, the vast majority of people you sell to are just as interested, or more interested, in the quality of your products and services than in the price. I've read many studies on the subject, talked to thousands of customers/prospects/buyers, and worked with the top people in selling, so please trust me on this! People consider the quality of what they are buying as equal to or greater than the importance of the actual price when they are making a buying decision.

I know that isn't what they say! I know it isn't what you hear out there! But it's true anyway. If what you are selling is of high quality, sell it from that position! If it isn't of high quality, start selling something that is. And then, from that position, you'll have your cake and be able to eat it too. Why? Because you can then sell quality and price! Remember: The price of a quality product is always lower over the long haul. See! The best is the cheapest!

Who?

Don't try this unless you are really good. It will work in any type of selling, but it is especially effective in telephone selling. Here's the setting: "Mr. Big" is a customer. He thinks, and rightly so, that the sun rises and sets on him. He thinks he has you by the financial throat. He wants better deals, lower prices, faster service, and anything else he can think of. Although he usually isn't, I picture him at about three hundred pounds, puffing on a black cigar, with a diamond pinky ring and alligator shoes.

The phone rings. Your receptionist tells you who it is, so by the time you pick up the phone you probably have his entire customer file up on the screen in front of you — *but don't let on!*

"Mr. Big" begins his normal blow-hard conversation. Just as he gets rolling, simply say **"I'm sorry, I didn't catch your name."** Pray he gives you just his last name. If he does, say **"And your first name?"** You will be stunned at the calming effect this has on that type of person. And if it's a relatively common name, you might even press further with something like, **"Thank you! We're getting closer now! And which company are *you* with?"**

Now keep it friendly, bright, and helpful! You aren't being arrogant, you're just a little "bewildered." And what you've done is gently inform him that he isn't nearly the big deal he thought he was. Then, when you *slowly* begin to recognize him with the little things you "suddenly remember" (i.e., "Don't you sell those little green widgets?" or "Aren't you a skier?"), he'll overreact with gratitude! He'll lick your hand! Recognition is *vital* to his mental health!

This beats the heck out of not being available when he calls, then calling back to gain the psychological advantage and all the other nonsense I hear in sales training sessions.

Among the best I've ever seen with this technique is one of the top automobile salespeople in the world. If you try to bowl him over, especially in front of a prospect or friend you've brought in to impress, you'll soon be spreading out your identification on the hood of a car — trying to prove you

217

really *are* a big deal, while he stares at you like an amnesia victim.

Remember: You always want to sell from a position of strength, so first you must be in one.

Repeat It!

My human behavioral scientist and psychologist-type friends tell me that the human brain is a little slow on the uptake — especially when it's receiving unsolicited material (such as *your* sales presentation!). Therefore, just as advertisers figure they have to show you an ad seven times before they begin to reach maximum mental impact, you should state each of the important benefits of your product three to four times in every sales presentation.

As a sales pro, you'll have to create three to four *different* ways to explain each benefit, so you won't sound as if you're repeating yourself. And don't get self-conscious and give up too soon! Just because you know what you're doing doesn't mean they do. In fact, you'll be lucky if it has registered even then!

Work on it! Find three or four different explanations for each of your product's best benefits and use them in every single sales presentation.

I *know* you'll remember to do this — I just told you **three times!**

Did I Hear an Order?

One of my favorite salespeople is Bob Tolbert. You may have talked with him when placing orders with Hampton Books. If you have, you know how smooth he is. But, strong as he is, one of the best things he does is so simple and soft it's devastating! It gets him orders no one else gets and, on those sales any good salesperson would eventually get, Bob gets them in half the time — sometimes in the very first few *seconds* of a presentation!

Here's how it goes: Bob begins his presentation and, as soon as he feels his prospect has enough information to *conceivably* make a positive decision to buy, his listening antennas go up. As soon as the prospect gives *any* positive reaction to *any* point, Bob just smiles and says, **"Was that a 'yes' I just heard?"** Bang! He often has an order while the rest of us are still introducing ourselves and swapping business cards.

And what if they say "no"? Bob just says "oh," and plunges on — waiting for the next positive grunt. Then he does it again . . . and again! Usually, by the time he's done it three or four times, both he and the prospect are good-naturedly enjoying the game. This leaves the prospect wide open for, **"So what's holding you back?"** And that either gets him a sale or a specific objection with which to deal. Either way, he wins!

What do you think? Was that a "yes" I just heard?

Do a Sammy Davis

With Lake Tahoe right up the road from our home, my wife and I used to love to watch Sammy Davis, Jr. perform. What a pro he was! He could sing. He could dance. He could tell great show business stories. He could mesmerize an audience. What he *didn't* do very well were imitations, a personal flaw he readily admitted. But since imitations are almost demanded from variety entertainers, he had to figure out a way around his weakness.

What did he do? When Sammy started to do James Cagney, for example, he would walk to the front of the stage and announce he was now doing James Cagney. The audience loved it!

Sammy said by doing it that way he had the audience on his side, and it cut down on people in the audience mumbling to each other, "Who's he doing now?" Professional speakers use the same technique — the good ones anyway. They tell the crowd what they are about to tell them. Then they tell them.

219

Then they tell them what they just told them. I call it a "Sammy Davis."

It works equally well in selling. Don't leave them wondering and apprehensive. Tell them why you are there, what you hope to accomplish, and why it will be of benefit to them. Tell them what you are going to tell them. Then tell them. Then tell them what you told them.

Want a strong lead-in for using this approach? I always tell them what I just told you — the Sammy Davis story. Feel free to use it!

Tuesdays Stink!

A weakness common to most salespeople, especially the weaker ones, is the belief that there are certain times of the day when you can't sell. Or of the week. Or of the month. Or of the year. Or even in entire sections of the country. Some folks really believe it!

Well, the top pros don't believe it. They *know* better! And they conduct themselves accordingly. So should you!

Here's an example I was personally involved in. For a variety of reasons, the mail in some parts of the country is lighter on Tuesdays. If you think about it, it makes sense. If most First Class mail takes two to three days to reach you, the mail you get on Tuesdays would probably have been mailed on a Saturday or Sunday. As you know, few businesses and few people mail on either of those two days. Hence the sometimes slow mail day on Tuesday.

The plot thickens: I began noticing a weird attitude among our salespeople. On Tuesdays they tended to arrive later, work less, and leave sooner. So, being naive, I asked what the problem was. Seems they had heard from the folks in the mail room that Tuesdays were always slow. A fact that was confirmed by the people in the Accounting Department, at least by those whose job it was to open the mail and extract the mail orders.

Get the picture? If so, you're quicker than I was! They almost had me going . . . until I discovered the secret of the Saturday and Sunday mailing days. And even then I had to show them on charts and graphs that, except for the lighter mail, Tuesdays were perfectly normal business days. In fact, they tended to be the second best day of the week!

Did that cure the problem? Sort of. But then they wanted to know what *was* the worst day. And the best day. And the best time of the year. And the . . .

Here's the answer: The top professional salespeople I know, the so-called Master Closers, all agree that the best time to sell is whenever you can get the undivided attention of a qualified prospect. And that means it could be at 2:30 AM on a Tuesday morning, in Des Moines, outside of a saloon, hanging upside down in a tree, during a national economic recession, in a hail storm.

Tuesdays don't stink, but I'll admit some salespeople stink on Tuesdays. And in the Spring. And on rainy days. And if they see a black cat. Don't become one of them!

Make Them Feel Good

People will spend money when they are sad — at a florist shop or in a funeral home. And they'll spend money when they are mad — in a lawyer's office.

They'll even spend money when they are scared — in a gun shop. But if you don't sell for one of those types of businesses, you are left with the only other time when they'll buy. When they are GLAD!

Understand this: There are only four basic individual categories of human emotional conditions. Don't let the sub-categories — and there are many of them — fool you. No matter what appears to be going on, people are either mad, scared, sad, or glad. Period. And, except for the unusual situations I mentioned before, they will only buy when they are GLAD!

So what is your job? To make *sure* they are glad! Glad about you. Glad about your product. Glad about its benefits. Glad to be doing business with you.

Contrary to popular opinion, people *love* to spend money. But they only enjoy doing it when and where they are happy (glad) and comfortable. It's your job to create, control, and maintain that atmosphere. At least that's what the wealthy salespeople do . . . and they are very glad about it!

From Copenhagen

The napkin this one came from would indicate it was from a conversation late one night in Copenhagen, Denmark. I was probably discussing the common characteristics of the very best salespeople in the world with a couple of old friends, Larry Nelson and Derek Broughton, two of the better salespeople I've ever had the privilege of working with.

Remember the old movies where a guy is driving a car? Out the rear window you see a moving picture of what he is supposedly driving past. Now close your eyes and picture his hands and the steering wheel.

What did you see? I'll bet you pictured the constant movement of the steering wheel. Back and forth, back and forth, about six inches each way. Right?

Now let's think about it for a moment. If you really drove a car that way you'd crash, or be pulled over for drunk driving! Except for going around corners, good driving isn't a series of constant visible moves, is it? Of course not! Good drivers use constant, but very slight, pressures. Smooth driving is a nuance. It's almost invisible to the naked eye!

When I was first taking flying lessons, I too had the movements of the old movie actors. I would jerk the plane into the air, careening to the right, careening to the left, and nosedive toward the runway like a man bent on suicide. I thought you were supposed to handle a plane like a steer wrestler handles steers at a rodeo.

Well, if you catch my drift, most salespeople sell like the actor used to drive and like I used to fly. They are constantly jerking the customer around, changing their sales presentations, trying new tactics at inopportune times, dropping things, forgetting things, and generally embarrassing themselves.

On the other hand, Messrs. Broughton, Nelson, and I had noticed that almost all of the top folks in selling share these admirable characteristics: They have seamless presentations. In other words, it's hard to find the breaks between the opening, the middle, and the close of their sales presentations. They don't make visible moves. They sell with constant slight pressures. They understand that selling isn't a series of thunderclaps and explosions. It is a beautiful ballet, a series of nuances.

In my wild youth, back when I had more money than brains, I was considering buying a Grand Mercedes. That was the old giant 600 series, like the Pope might cruise around in. It was magnificent — all six doors of it! Well anyway, I was absolutely amazed at its quietness. It made my brand new Cadillac sound like a dragster by comparison!

So the salesman takes me out for a demonstration ride and we start down the road toward my home. He pulled over, said he wanted to demonstrate something, and asked me to close my eyes. He made me promise not to open them again until he told me to. Several minutes went by and, except for a few nervous laughs and questions from me, there wasn't a sound or movement in the car. Then he said to open my eyes.

There we were, still sitting by the side of North San Pedro Road. The only difference being that we were two miles farther down North San Pedro Road than we had been when I first shut my eyes! I hadn't felt or heard a thing!

It was a wonderful tribute to the quality of the automobile and to his ability to start, drive, and stop it so smoothly and evenly. I've often thought of that drive when I was trying to do something smoothly and gracefully — like give a professional sales presentation.

Make a note! Selling at the highest levels is almost invisible. It's a series of quiet, smooth, and very slight pressures. Top professional selling is a subtle series of delicate nuances. And, if they can see you doing it, you aren't doing it right! At least that's what three of us decided one night in Copenhagen.

Uh, Houston . . .

Depending on how old you are, you may know the rest of that famous phrase with little or no prompting. It's one of the best examples I know to demonstrate the value of prior preparation and constant, continuing training, whether you are in selling or any other career.

The timeframe is during the days of the Apollo program, NASA's manned missions to the moon. Apollo 11 landed safely on the moon, as did Apollo 12. Then Apollo 13 took off, got about halfway to the moon, and the back end of it blew off! It was a potential disaster of enormous proportions!

Picture it. Three astonauts stranded in space. Doomed to die and spend eternity circling the moon and the earth. A modern-day version of mythical ghost ships of old.

Knowing those dire consequences, how would you have reacted to the sound of the sudden explosion in the dark vacuum of deep space? Well, thanks to years of prior preparation and training, the reaction that traveled through space that horrible day was the soft Southern drawl of a highly trained and well-prepared astronaut. With less reaction than I have when I miss a short putt, he said, "Uh, Houston — we've got a problem here."

How does this apply to you and me? Forget astronauts. Forget Apollo. Remember *training* and *prior preparation.* And remember when it is done. You don't practice how to overcome a sudden sales emergency during an actual sales presentation. If you're smart, you do it IN ADVANCE. Just like the astronauts, you role play every conceivable selling situation IN ADVANCE. Remember, there is nothing terribly unique or different about your products, your services, your customers, your prospects — or you, for that matter (sorry about that!).

Practice! Role play! Practice! Role play! Practice! Role play! Yes, I know. You don't want to do it. Neither do I! Neither does anyone else I know! But ALL the real sales pros do it anyway. Again and again and again. Until the proper responses are as automatic as breathing.

Let me be blunt. People who enter selling, potentially the highest paid profession on earth, and expect to get rich with a smile, a warm handshake, and a shoeshine are ignorant beyond belief. They were the kids in school who didn't do their homework, didn't study for tests, cut classes, and then prayed for A's. It didn't work then, it won't work now. Here's a goal: Do your sales presentation so well that no matter what occurs during a selling situation — no matter what — you will be able to smile inwardly, maintain your blood pressure at a constant level and say to yourself, "Uh, Houston . . . we've got a problem here." And then, using all of that prior practice, solve the problem, close the sale, collect the payment, and go home. By the way, that's what the crew of Apollo 13 did. They came home.

Here Lies You

Here's a quick one, but it's good food for thought:

I'm sitting in a sales meeting one Saturday morning about 25 years ago. Bill Dempsey and Jimmy Rucker are conducting it for their sales organizations. They are doing all the usual stuff when Dempsey suddenly says, "O.K., you all just died of heart attacks! They are going to take your body to the salespeople's graveyard for burial. You get to write your own salesperson's epitaph for your tombstone . . . and being salespeople, it can be as long and as flowery as you wish, but it must be only about your own sales career. Write it the way you really want it to turn out. Start writing now."

There was a flurry of writing all around the room. In the beginning there was some joking and laughter, but the salespeople quickly settled down to a serious writing project. About ten minutes later everyone had finished. Someone asked if they should turn them in, but Dempsey replied, "No. It's not important that I know what you wrote. It's only important that you know. Now, from this day forward, do everything possible to make yourself worthy of the sales epitaph you just wrote."

That moment has stuck with me all these years. It's a psychologically sound premise — being able to visualize and internalize your own personal future. Then, through hard work, making it manifest itself into reality. I recommend you do the exercise too.

Yep, I wrote mine that day. That original sheet of paper is still in my tickler file almost a quarter of a century later and I look at it every Monday morning. Am I there yet? Not quite, but I'm getting closer by the day!

Let 'Em See It!

All of the big-time sales pros I know have the ability to help their customers see (visualize) the product or service they sell and, of course, the benefits it will bring. They can put their customers "in the picture," letting them experience mentally now what they will enjoy physically at a later time. When it is done well, it is both an art _and_ a science. If you want to be a big-time sales pro, you're going to have to develop this selling skill fully.

Some of you have the benefit of selling things the client can physically experience during the sales presentation. For instance, if you sell cars, or property, or riding lawn mowers, it isn't difficult to see how you can put them in the picture and get them actively involved. But you must still work on your descriptive language! Even with live demonstrations, salespeople who talk in Technicolor sell about 20% more than those who only speak in black and white — with all else being equal.

And some of you sell heavily documented products or services. By that I mean, you have beautiful descriptive literature available. Or audio/video demonstrations to use. This is second best to live demonstrations, so it is even more important that you become a vivid, interesting, believing spokesperson for your product. If you do, you can expect to make about 25% more than someone who isn't — all else being equal.

But what about those of you who don't have live demonstrations to work with and haven't been provided with dazzling literature or multimedia light shows? And what about those of you who spend a good deal of time selling on the phone? Well, for you the difference is extreme. Now we aren't talking about 20–25% one way or the other, we are talking about whether you remain in selling or not! And, just as an aside, virtually every one of you is going to be spending a great deal of time on the phone in the future — if not all of it!

So what do you do? As you'll recall, we've covered — and will cover again — descriptive phrasing. You must learn to put the beauty, the colors, the drama, the power, and the size of the Grand Canyon into your language. You'll sell few tour tickets to see it if you just say it is a large ditch. Even though, in fact, that's all it is!

I want you to write down, practice, and memorize colorful ways to describe your product or service's features and benefits to others. One of the best salespeople I know, a beautiful Southern belle, does it this way: When she receives a new product or service to sell she studies it thoroughly. She gets excited about it (or refuses to sell it). She writes down, practices, and memorizes colorful ways to describe the features and benefits it offers. Then when she is sure she is ready, she blindfolds her loyal, trusting husband and begins fine-tuning her new sales presentation. And she stays at it until her husband, a fellow sales heavyweight, can visualize it and wants it — without ever having seen it! Are you up to that?

If you spend time on the phone, it is *mandatory* that you have the actual products there with you. If size or cost prohibits that, you must have descriptive literature and color pictures in sight *at all times!* No matter how familiar you are with an object, it is always easier to describe it if you are holding or looking at one. That's just plain common sense, right?

And now, for additional believability, learn to add further phrases like, "I've got one right here. I'm holding it in my hand and . . ."

Or you might say, "I'm looking at a photograph of it as I'm talking to you and . . ."

Or try, "This isn't theory to me. I've got a sample in my hands but, more importantly, I have one of my own at home! Let me tell you . . ."

Or maybe, "I had the privilege of touring the factory recently. I've actually watched the care and craftsmanship that goes into every one they make. Let me describe . . ."

Here's a side benefit of handling the product while

you're selling: You'll see things you've never seen before, or you'll discover better and better ways to describe features and benefits you thought had been described to death. They'll jump out at you when you are least expecting it!

What's the hardest part of this skill I want you to develop? Getting your husband or wife to put on the blindfold!

What Are They Saying About You?

From time to time I'm asked to find out why a salesperson or a group of salespeople is succeeding or failing. The object being to replicate the successes in others and/or to discover the problems and weaknesses, so they can be eliminated immediately and avoided in the future.

My favorite half of that type of job is finding out why people are succeeding. And my favorite method for doing it, when the situation allows, is to talk with past and present customers.

Not too long ago I was asked to provide this service for one of the best salespeople I know. Guess who asked me to do it . . . and guess who paid for it?

If you guessed the salesperson himself, you're right . . . and we are starting to make some real progress! See, the top folks want to know how they're doing, so they can do more of the good stuff and less of the bad!

Well anyway, I talked to about 45 of his past and present customers. I had extremely blunt conversations with them (after they were assured of complete anonymity) and here's a composite of what they said. Now pay attention. My client is one of the very best. It is to your selfish advantage to know what he does. If you can emulate his performance, your bank account can then emulate his bank account!

First, the only significant criticism I heard: They don't see enough of him! They wish he would come by more often.

He is a bright spot in their lives, brimming with new ideas to help them. They want more of his time. They wish there were two of him!

How would you like to hear that said about you? That's significantly different from having them not return phone calls, right? Or having them draw the curtains and turn out the lights when you turn into the driveway!

And now the good stuff, remembering that this is the composite response of about 45 customers:

They said they enjoyed giving my client business because he was always totally honest with them — to the point of being very blunt. And he was as blunt about his own products' weaknesses as he was about their strengths! They said they liked the fact that he was well-informed, but not a know-it-all. That he asked intelligent questions and *listened* to the answers.

Further, they liked the focus and attention he put on their needs. They regarded him as a full member of their team, not an outsider who needed to be watched every second. And they liked the fact that, through him, they had the full use of the resources of his entire company working for them — at no charge!

They said he never wasted their time with old, worn-out ideas. Rather, the mere sight of him meant good news and higher profits. And they said they would be honored to have him as a personal friend.

If you wanted to design a model salesperson, that description would certainly be a good place to start. Then, if you can build from there, going to even higher plateaus of excellence, we'll soon be writing chapters, or whole books, about YOU!

Note: Not one single customer mentioned how many tricky closes my client used on them, but that was probably an oversight — right?

Some or All?

I know a man who isn't the brightest person who ever lived. We aren't talking rocket scientist here. And he isn't terribly articulate. Nor is he even average in appearance. Yet he is consistently among the top producers in a rather large direct sales organization. Has been for many years.

I took him to dinner one night after an awards ceremony I had emceed for his company. A ceremony where he won just about every award except Rookie of the Year! After we chatted for a while he said, "Well, go ahead. Ask me." I said, "Ask you what?" And he said, "Ask me how a homely guy with no education, no class, no style, and no real chance for success made it anyway. Go ahead, ask me." So I did.

He said, "I get up early and I work late. I call on lots of people. I know my products, believe in them, and guarantee them personally. I ask everyone who listens to my presentation to buy my products. And I do it clearly, where there is no misunderstanding of my intentions. I'm turned down frequently — about 40% of the time. But I discovered early on that those who don't ask for the order are turned down 100% of the time — so, by asking for the order every single time, I face 60% less rejection than the others do. That's it. I'm sorry. I have no secret to share with you." I'm sure you'll agree, he was *totally wrong* on that last point!

I Know What Your Customers Want!

I've quoted the adage "Find a need and fill it" more times than you probably want to hear it, but it remains one of the great truths in selling nonetheless. So, when your Widget Model #1322-B fills a customer's wants or needs, it doesn't take a high-powered sales pro to complete the sale. Assuming it's priced competitively, it really only takes exposure to financially qualified prospects, right?

But what are the wants and needs customers are always trying to fill, whether Widget Model #1322-B fits the bill or not? In other words, what "magic" needs do the top sales pros seem to find time and time again, even when there isn't such a clear cut relationship of want/need/problem to product/service/solution?

Well, whether they can quote them verbatim or not, the pros all seem to understand innately that all people constantly share certain basic wants and needs. And that people spend their entire lives trying to satisfy those basic wants and needs. And that those basic wants and needs are *never* satisfied completely. Phrased differently, your prospects have incurable cases of poison ivy of their human wants and needs systems. Just like scratching an itch, you can solve these special generic needs and wants for a few minutes, maybe even for a day, but the problem always returns quickly. And, because it returns, you have an almost inexhaustible opportunity to continue solving an individual's wants and needs! In fact, you are limited only by the range of your products and services, by your imagination, and by your ability to communicate.

What are these magic inexhaustible wants and needs you'll grow old and rich trying to fill? Get out your highlighter pen and I'll tell you:

All people you will ever meet are in constant search for **recognition**. They want and need to be recognized for their achievements, their purchases, their investments, their families, their jobs, their cars, their houses, etc., etc. Find ways to help them gain recognition and you are well on your way to the top!

All the people you will ever meet have a strong need or want to be **respected**. This is similar to their need for recognition, but it is harder to fill. The good news is, once filled, it tends to last longer and needs less maintenance. Find ways to help them gain respect in the eyes of others and, more importantly, in their own eyes, and you are closer to your own goals (wants and needs).

All of the people you will ever meet have a want or need to experience a feeling of **pride**. They want to do things, to participate in things, to achieve things that make them swell with pride. To feel proud of themselves. Fill that one on a regular basis and you'll be rich!

All of the people you will ever meet want to make good decisions, **to be right** on issues, to do the right things. They want the feeling of personal security brought on by correct and proper choices. Help them "be right" and they'll help you succeed!

All of the people you will ever meet have basic fears that there are **better ways to do things** they are already doing — methods they are not aware of. They want those feelings to go away! It's the reason they buy so many "how-to" books and tapes and attend so many seminars! Discover what they are doing now, show them a better way to accomplish the same or even better results, provide the product or service to do it, then start shopping for that cabin by the lake you've always wanted.

All people you will ever meet want to **belong**. They want to belong to special groups, to special companies, to special families, to special groups of owners. Help them belong to groups of special individuals — people of achievement, people of accomplishment, people of distinction, people of means. Help them become members and you, in turn, will join a select group of sales professionals — the wealthy ones!

And two last categories: These are the twin umbrellas that, in a broad general manner, cover *all* wants and *all* needs. Everything you ever learn about human emotion, about what makes people tick, always boils down to just two things. They all have **hope of reward** as a result of their actions. And they all want to **avoid losing** what they already have when they take action. Remember: hope of reward or fear of loss (or both) is the ultimate reasoning people will use when deciding whether or not to buy or not buy from you.

To recap: The human wants and needs that need filling like a bottomless pit are:

1. **recognition**
2. **respect**
3. **pride**
4. **to be right**
5. **to do better**
6. **to belong**
7. **to be rewarded**
8. **to not lose**.

Build your sales career around these psychological human truths as a vine entwines a tree, and you'll rise to the top in selling as sure as the sun rises in the east and sets in the west.

Which One Do You Want?

You know the old saying, "If life gives you a lemon, make lemonade!" Well, a friend of mine sells swimming pools. She's one of the best I've ever watched work. She sells her pools in Marin County, which is in Northern California and happens to be one of the wealthiest counties in the nation.

The economic strata she sells in is made up of people who are, generally speaking, well-educated, conservative, financially secure, and careful with their purchases and investments. My friend, however, is a delightful, bubbly blabbermouth. No amount of training has been able to cure her tendency to talk too much, give too many details, and point out too may features. But by the same token, I must admit she does tend to cover *lots* of benefits along the way!

Trust me when I say we *could not* get her to shut up! No matter how many sales she lost by talking her way past the close, she persisted. She is a "talk-aholic"!

That's the lemon. Where's the lemonade? Simple! We

built a special close to complement her admitted weakness.

First, we got her to recognize the problem. Then we got her to spot when she was actually doing it. Then we encouraged her to go two or three major benefits *past* that point! And then we trained her to stop and say (in her best Southern drawl), "Oh, I'm so, so sorry! I'm telling you more than you want to know, aren't I? I'll be quiet. Which one do you want?"

That's it! And she's tops in her field! So whether you do it deliberately or on purpose, when you find yourself way out on that limb we talkative types tend to spend so much time on, just stop and say, "I'm sorry! I'm telling you more than you want to know, aren't I? I'll be quiet. Which one do you want?"

A client in Waterville, Maine puts an additional twist on it. He says, "I'm sorry! I'm telling you more than you want to know, aren't I? Forgive me! It's just that I love this [product] so much! I'll be quiet. Which one do you want?"

Got a selling weakness? Everyone does! I've got more than my share, I assure you! So cure them one at a time and/or build special phrases and closes that work with and complement them. But I'm telling you more than you want to know, aren't I? I'll be quiet. Which way do you want to do it?

Be Brave!

You say your company won't give you the sales support you need? You say you're a top-notch sales closer and your time should be spent talking to top-of-the-line customers? You say your income is being cut in half because of the wasted time you have to spend on piddling details and small accounts? Good news! If you're strong, this section will solve your problem — assuming you're at least semi-brave, and assuming you're already doing reasonably well financially.

The first solution that comes to most salespeople's minds is to change jobs. To go to that great company across town that handles all this trivial stuff for their salespeople. But here's the inside scoop: Their salespeople are looking at your company with envy! It's the old "greener grass" problem all over again!

So stay right where you are, but note what a Master Closer friend of mine from Warren, Massachusetts did to solve the same problem:

He was already a making a lot of money the day he asked me to show him how he could make a lot more. Although we can always improve, his sales presentations and closing skills were already excellent. He is a sales pro in the finest sense of the word. So we'd have to find some other area to radically improve if we were going to significantly increase his income.

For starters, I put a person on his tail for two solid weeks. She met him bright and early at his front door every morning and stayed with him until the last working minute every evening. And she kept detailed notes regarding the use of his time. She charted how much time he actually spent selling — and to whom. How much time he spent setting up appointments. How much time he spent filling out reports. How much time he spent with smaller, less profitable accounts, and how much with the high-ticket, high-profit ones. How much time was just wasted completely, and so on.

His final report showed that we had a high-powered sales closing machine on our hands, but one who spent only 3 hours and 10 minutes out of every 10-hour day in a "closing situation" where a potential sale was at least theoretically possible. If that shocks you, chart your own selling day. I seriously doubt it will top his 31%. It's probably *significantly* less!

So the solution appeared simple. I'd just go to his boss, who happened to be a very good friend of mine, show him how much time and talent was being wasted, and he'd hire someone to work directly with and assist this sales dynamo. The new person would handle the details that were cluttering up the selling day and we'd all live happily ever after. No such luck!

Does, "If we did that for him, we'd have to do it for

everyone!" sound familiar? Well, the discussion took about two hours, but that was the long and short of it. So what should we do about this?

Telling them they were about to lose their top gun gave me a little leverage, so I was able to swing this deal:

My sales dynamo needed about 150 square feet of office space in which to work our "sales support team" concept, so he *leased* it from his employer. Then he furnished it! Then he became an independent agent and set up his own sales consulting corporation, working on straight commission. Then *he* hired a sharp assistant who immediately began taking all of the non-productive, non-selling chores off his hands. How could he afford to do this? Easy! He *fired* the person who had been doing it and who had been charging fifteen times as much per hour! Who was this terrible villain? **Himself!**

Now get this! Before he really got into gear . . . before he really began to trust his assistant enough to leave her totally alone and tend only to his job of selling . . . before any of this really kicked in . . . he increased his selling time to 6 hours per day, from the previous 3 hours and 10 minutes!

The story gets better! Even under this system, he was spending too much time with small accounts, and they still weren't getting enough attention. Solution? The first step had worked so well, he took a deep breath and went to Stage 2. He hired a marginal salesperson away from his own former employer, with their enthusiastic permission, of course, trained him to sell and "order-take" primarily via telephone, sent out letters of introduction and turned over 400 smaller accounts to him. This man's job is to handle all routine incoming orders, while phoning 40 established customers a day — just taking their pulse, picking up standard reorders, telling them of specials, etc. Under this system, the smaller accounts are all contacted every two weeks. Under the old system, months went by with NO contact!

My sales dynamo is now something to watch. Unless he *wants* to do something just for therapy, he spends hardly any time doing anything but what he does best — selling! He doesn't pick up laundry anymore, or fill out sales reports, or handle petty office disputes, or swap stories with unproductive salespeople who have lots of time on their hands. *He sells!*

When he gets up in the morning, he looks at his assistant's neatly typed daily sales schedule. He hits the front door, picks up his cellular phone, checks in, and he's out doing what he does best — selling!

If he has a shipping or inventory problem, he tells his assistant to solve it. He keeps doing what he does best. He sells!

Hospitals don't ask brain surgeons to mop the operating room floor, or count the scalpels, or order sheets and towels. They set up a system where the brain surgeon does what he or she does best — brain surgery!

So you want to be a Master Closer? Well, stop counting the paper clips. Stop filling out meaningless forms! Stop spending all day today setting up tomorrow. Do what you do best — sell! And if that's not possible with your current set-up, change your set-up!

George Bernard Shaw said, "The people who get on in this world are the people who get up and look for the circumstances they want and, if they can't find those circumstances, *they make them!"*

Buy a Pair of Scissors

Ever had a smart salesperson or a friend (which could conceivably be the same person!) send you a magazine, newspaper article, or even a book with a "Thought of you when I read this" note? If the article fits the recipient, it's a tremendously effective way to endear yourself to someone! But, for some strange reason, hardly anyone does it anymore. And that's where you, the Master Closer, come in!

Remember, before the Army and Marines go ashore, the artillery softens the target. As in warfare, the object in selling is to make it as easy and painless as possible. The sales stories of knocked down, dragged out, jarring confrontations with customers make for great legends, _if_ they resulted in sales, but all they really prove is that someone did a poor job to begin with, that the salesperson was an amateur at everything in selling except for the bloody final showdown . . . or make that shakedown!

Most of the good sales books, tapes, and seminars tell you to look for interesting articles, clip them out, add a personal note, and send them to customers who would enjoy reading them. So this isn't new to you, is it? Then why aren't you sending out at least 20 or 30 a week? It would make you a lot more sales, I sincerely promise you!

I'll bet this is why: Without a simple, easy-to-use system, it looks like a fruitless project. Like emptying the ocean with a teaspoon. Hopeless!

Well, help has arrived, thanks to a Master Closer friend from Pasadena, California. He is a Master Closer because, among other things, he is a master at staying in touch with his clients, friends, and business associates. And he does it all with clippings and brief personal notes — usually just an "Enjoy!" or "Thought of you!" written on the photocopy of the article. And they are always in _hand-addressed_ envelopes, usually written "on the run" — or so he makes it appear.

So how is he able to do something you and I find so insurmountable? Easy! I call it programmed warmth. When you first meet him, he takes one of your business cards. Before he forgets, he writes a number or two on the back of your card. That number(s) puts you in a category or two of people he deals with. Yes, my friend has broken down the entire human race into just twenty-five categories!

When he returns to the office, he adds you to the list or

lists you qualified to be on. For instance, you might be on list #1 (salespeople) and list #14 (food & wine connoisseurs), or lists #2 and #17, or lists #9 and #20, or whatever. And, judging by the notes I get from him (about two a month), some of us must be on even more than two lists!

O.K., that's Step 1. Now, with the twenty-five categories in the back of his mind, he simply reads many newspapers and magazines every month. Whenever he sees an article of interest to people in one or more of his categories, he clips it out, makes the appropriate number of copies, tosses that many envelopes and stamps in his briefcase, and, during downtime (on airplanes, in waiting rooms, etc.), he addresses envelopes, adds personal notes, seals them, stamps them, and drops them in the nearest mailbox. I've had warm notes and informative articles from all over the world!

What if he sends you something you've already seen? So what? It's the *thought* that counts! And I think of him every single time I need his type of service. I've sent *dozens* of new customers to him over the years! See? He has programmed me to think almost exclusively of him when his type of service is mentioned.

Here's a side benefit he enjoys from this constant contact with his customers and associates: He doesn't have to use tricky closes on us! The opposite is true. We usually call him and try to get a spot on his busy schedule.

By the way, he sends out about 10,000 personally noted articles a year. Before you choke, that's only about twenty-eight a day! Time involved? About twenty minutes of time that would have been wasted anyway! And the cost? Figure a stamp, an envelope, and a photocopy. Then figure he says the return is about twenty-fold per year in cash and a hundredfold in personal pleasure!

So whether you do it with the help of a computer, a tickler file, or a pile of yellow pads, get with the program! By the way, think of me when you see articles that people on lists #1, 14, 18, 21 and 24 would enjoy. My address is in this book!

Curing the "Be-Back" Blues

Roland Madden is one of those top sales pros I frequently refer to. At this writing, he is the sales manager for one of the major timeshare/resort sales organizations in the world. Anyway, Roland's industry is plagued with people who will "be back" to buy after they "think it over," "check out some other places," "talk to Uncle Harry," etc., etc.

One day he had a flash of inspiration just as a couple was announcing they'd be back to buy later. He whipped out his wallet, pulled out a hundred dollar bill and said, "Hey, that's great! Now as you know, the resort won't be able to give you all of the gifts, bonuses, and extras you'd earn if you joined our family today — but I want to do something for you personally. I'm going to give you this one hundred dollar bill on the day you actually return and finalize the ownership we've been discussing. Here, just initial it somewhere on the bill and I'll hold it for you — until you come back." It worked like a charm! The couple sat there for a few moments, then smiled, and the husband said, "Roland, you're so right. If we don't do it now, we'll never do it. Let's fill out the paperwork!" Was that a fluke? Not really. Roland tells me that out of every one thousand "be-backs" in his industry, only three couples actually return and make a purchase. And how many does he get with his hundred dollar bills? He isn't saying! But I can tell you that Roland is a legend at his local bank. That's where he takes his bills for replacement after they're filled up with initials. They're a sight to behold!

And that brings me to the last part of Roland Madden's "be-back" cure. He uses the **same bill** over and over again, until there is zero room for new initials. Why? Because that makes people ask why there are so many other initials on it, to which he replies, "Oh, those are other nice folks just like you who said they'd be back too. But they haven't yet and, because the prices have risen so much since they initialed my bill, they probably can't afford to now. Realistically it's sort of now or never. It's really a shame."

Can you feel it? Is it any wonder Roland has slashed his "be-back" problem to the bone?

Final tip: Don't let them initial over the serial number on the bill. The bank won't redeem it if you do!

Zero In!

And while I'm in my Roland Madden note file, here's another super cure he uses for the "I've-got-to-think-it-over" stall. If you aren't selling timeshares, memberships, and/or resort property, just give it some thought and you'll come up with something that works equally well with your product or service!

The couple announces that they've enjoyed the tour, are very interested, will be back (there it is again!), but just want to think it over for a while. To which Roland replies, "I understand. You know it reminds me of something my old baseball coach told our team years ago. He said not to get confused by all the rules and regulations. There were only three things really going on in a baseball game: You throw. You hit. You catch. That's it!

"And that's the way it is here. There are only three things involved with your timeshare ownership. You own it. You use it. You exchange it. Now which of those do you really need to think over?"

POW! They either come up with the thing that's bothering them or Roland now has license to say, "Well, is it _____? Or is it _____? Or, perhaps, is it _____?" And he's right back on track!

Remember, zero in! You can't overcome vague, hazy objections and stalls. You have to find out *exactly* what's holding them back, so you can provide the precise solution to the sales block.

Mr. Smooth

I constantly hammer on the need for you to learn how to sell from the customer's point of view. To become a member of his/her team before you even *attempt* to offer products or services that solve the problems at hand. Now I've got a new method of measuring how effective you've become at this learned skill. True story!

Here's the scene: I've got an old friend who has permission to walk into my office at any time — no matter what's going on. I have no secrets he isn't privy to. And I, in turn, feel equally comfortable walking into his office. As a result, we have each sat in on a lot of meetings or parts of meetings while waiting for the other one to get free for lunch, golf, or whatever.

About a year ago I'm meeting with a salesman from one of our suppliers. And this particular salesman is very good — a Master Closer. In fact, I've given you some of his stuff elsewhere in this book. Anyway, about 30 minutes before we ended our session, my friend walked in, waved, and flopped down on the couch. Pretending to read a magazine, I saw that he was really listening to the conversation I was having with the salesman.

The meeting ends. The salesman leaves. My friend and I head out for an early dinner. In the car my friend says, "That guy was really sharp. I haven't seen him around before. Which department does he work in?"

If you caught the real significance of that simple question, you are on the road to sales success! See, my friend, a top salesman in his own right, sat in on a meeting, listened carefully for 30 minutes, was impressed enough to ask about the man, but didn't realize he worked for another company and was actually calling on us!

Further discussion revealed that my friend thought the man and I had been working jointly on an internal problem and that, after we clearly defined it, planned to locate an outside supplier to purchase the solution. He couldn't believe the man *was* the outside supplier!

And that's your ultimate test in this type of selling. Get so good that an independent observer, even a skilled salesperson, could watch you work and not be sure whether you were the customer or the salesperson — until after the deal is closed!

Is It Really Real?

Here's a quick one that's worth the price of the whole book. One of my early mentors, the late great Walter Wells, used it effectively for years!

Walter was a master at giving a good solid presentation. He left no stone unturned. No edge of the carpet un-nailed. No door left open. When he decided it was time to ask for the order, believe me — it was time to ask for the order! He knew it. You knew it. You see, Walter, being a real sales pro, did the hard work up front. The close was just the logical, inevitable conclusion to the meeting.

But there are those times that, no matter what you do, no matter how careful you've been, your customers still pop up with some unexpected objection or delay. Well, if you've done your front work as well as Walter used to do his, you have license to use this. Walter would look at you. He'd smile kindly. He'd shake his head gently. He'd lean forward. He'd stare intently into your eyes. And then, very softly — like a kind old grandfather — he'd say, "Are you really serious? Or are you just testing my sales ability?"

You've got to be good and strong to use it at all but, if you qualify on that count, let me give you some encouraging news. I personally watched Walter use that no less than a hundred times, and can't remember it failing to close the sale more than five times! If you've got a final close that'll work 95% of the time, *share it with me!*

Warning: *Never use this final close unless and until you've earned the right to use it in an individual selling situation! If you've covered everything, and I mean everything, it'll work. But, if you use it when you haven't earned the right, you'll just look like a silly wise guy.*

Let Go!

Sooner or later I'm gonna getcha! I'm going to convert you into the type of salesperson who sells from the customer's side of the table. One who understands that selling isn't an armed conflict or a contact sport. As you've probably noticed, I tend to raise the issue rather regularly. I'm confident you understand it intellectually; the challenge is to get you to *feel it* emotionally. Here's a word picture to help you make the leap of faith over the chasm. Jimmy Rucker shared it with me many years ago.

Jimmy was having trouble getting a young salesman to sell with empathy. Finally the kid said, "Oh, I get it! Like an Indian! You want me to walk a mile in their moccasins before I try to sell them!" Jimmy replied, "Yes, but before you can walk that mile in *their* moccasins, you have to take *your* moccasins completely off!"

That make it clearer? Well, whether it does or not, do it! Let go! Like Billy Graham said at all those crusades, "Whether you understand it or not, I want you to get up out of your chairs and come down here. Take a leap of faith. Do it now. Don't let this moment pass."

Sell From the Audience

All of the magnificent performers I know — whether they are in show business, sales, law, or any other profession — have a special view of the world. I'm convinced it's one of the major elements of their greatness. Some have it unconsciously, others are always consciously and acutely aware of it, others can turn it on and off whenever they wish, like a television set. What is it? Psychologists call it the "fourth-wall perspective."

Here's the quickest way to explain it. Picture yourself at a play. Look at the stage. Assuming the scene is indoors, you are looking at the actors and they are enveloped by three walls: the rear wall and the ones on either side of the stage. But that's not the way it is in real life, is it? No, in real life there would be a fourth wall — the one opposite the rear wall. So where is the fourth wall? In a play, it's invisible, but it runs across the front of the stage. It's what the audience "looks through" when they watch the play.

All great salespeople I know are performers. Whether they are loud, quiet, aggressive, or laid back, they are always "on." They are always performing. They are aware of their surroundings — the surroundings anyone can plainly see (the three-wall view) *and* the view that can only be seen from the fourth-wall perspective. Yes, the truly great salespeople I know can mentally leave a sales presentation (or a meeting, or a lunch, or a casual conversation), go to another place, and look back as if from the audience — while it's going on!

At the risk of sounding spooky, they have what some might call "out-of-body experiences." And they use them productively because, in selling, we don't have the luxury of being coached by a director, producer, script girl, or teleprompter.

I know a man who specializes in group closes. From the front of the room, he sells packages worth thousands of dollars each. And he does it without ever having a private, one-on-one conversation with anyone in the audience. Just sheer selling power from the lectern!

His average audience runs about 500 people (250 couples), and his closing ratio holds steady at around 68% and has for years! In other words, he makes approximately 170 individual sales at an average presentation — having talked for about two and a half hours at each one.

While that's certainly amazing, it really isn't the amazing part! The amazing part comes in his hotel suite when, after each session, he literally dissects his latest performance with a few trusted friends and associates. I've sat in on several of these sessions over the years and not once have I heard him make an observation that sounded as if it was based on his physical view from the lectern looking out towards the audience. He sees the room and everything going on in it from the back of the room, and from the middle and from the sides. He views himself and his selling performance from the fourth-wall perspective, almost as if he was some alien viewing a laboratory experiment in a glass jar.

As you try to develop this skill, let me give you some motivation and inspiration. I've seen this man make more in commissions in one afternoon than the majority of salespeople make in a year. And he credits most of his closing ability to his fourth-wall perspective.

But you don't do group closes? Your office has a fourth wall! Your customers' offices have fourth walls! Your car has a fourth wall! All restaurants have fourth walls! And your telephone! And that empty building lot! All of life has a "fourth wall" to look through! Master Closers know where it is. Find yours quickly and you'll see the difference.

Straight-Straight

I had a breakthrough in selling one afternoon in Raleigh, North Carolina. Let me share it with you. It changed my entire sales career for the better. Hopefully, it will do the same for you!

I was working for a manufacturer's representative organization, George Friesem and Associates, and it was early in what was beginning to look like an unsuccessful endeavor for me in my sales career. To say the least, I was off to a slow start. It was, in fact, almost imperceptible!

So I'm riding along with the boss himself that fateful day, and he asks me what's holding me back. As you can imagine, the list was long and pitiful. But among the petty problems were two serious ones — for me at least. I was having trouble facing the price objection I knew was coming (we sold high-priced, high-quality items), and I dreaded actually asking for the order at the end.

George said that he had a solution for both problems, and that he'd do the next presentation for me. Well, we walk in, introduce ourselves, and sit down. And, before the buyer could say anything, George says, "Since I've never had the opportunity to work with you before, I'd like to explain how we operate right up front. We call it 'Straight-Straight.' You be straight with me and I'll be straight with you. You and I both know you don't have to buy from me — you have many other options open to you. And I have no control over your wants, your needs, or your order book. So I'd just like to establish a basic working agreement for this call and for all the calls Ben will make in the future. We'll simply show you the lines of merchandise we represent. If you see items that will help you, that you really want and need, I'll give you the very best possible pricing we have without any haggling. Then you tell me if it fits into your budget and, if so, we'll ship it to you whenever and wherever you want. Fair enough?"

I was amazed! The process I was using was so difficult and this suddenly seemed so easy!

Did we get an order? Yes. How big was it? I really don't recall, but I do remember it was all the customer wanted, needed, could reasonably use and afford. In other words, it was exactly the right size, *for the customer!* Anything more would have been just loading him up!

When we got back in the car, George said, "Now we've accomplished two things here today. First, we got a nice order. Second, just like a good well, you can return to this customer many times in the future — right up until the day you dump garbage in and ruin it. Do you understand?"

I'm sure I said I did. I'm equally sure I really didn't. Oh sure, I understood it intellectually. I could repeat it. But it took longer to absorb it, believe it, and use it on a daily basis. However, when Straight-Straight selling really got into my system, I was off and running!

You see, unless you are a charlatan, you only want to sell your customers what they want and/or need and can afford. Anything else is a con job. Yes, it is your job to help "create" new wants and needs. And yes, it's your job to help them think of ways they can afford to pay for them. But, if after all that, they either don't want it and/or need it, or can't afford to pay for it, you have *nothing* to discuss. So why not say that right up front? George did and he retired rich!

Cut Cancellations

Whatever you call cancelled orders in your business — chargebacks, dropouts, cancellations, etc. — it amounts to the same thing: lost income. And if the problem becomes severe enough, it can spell the end of your sales career.

I know of an industry where a cancellation rate of over 60% is considered normal! And I know some high-pressure, low-quality salespeople whose individual cancellation records are even higher than that!

Why? Well, some salespeople are simply selling high-pressure scams. For them, I hope their cancellation rate soon reaches 100%! But for the rest of us, higher-than-normal drop-out rates are usually easy to cure with but a few simple remedies. Let me give you the best example of a "problem and cure" case study I know.

I was doing the sales training for a large direct sales organization. Over the years they had discovered that a 5% cancellation rate was acceptable — *even desirable!* Seems that anyone who didn't have a 5% cancellation wasn't pressing hard enough, but anything significantly over 5% reflected another problem — usually too much pressure, or too little something else.

The specific problem we had came in the form of a tall, handsome young dynamo. Mark (not his real name) was writing more new business than just about anyone in the company. In this organization that meant he was usually number one or two out of thousands of salespeople across the nation. But that was only in gross sales. By the time his cancellations and chargebacks came in, he was usually back in the middle of the pack — on a net basis, he was just an average, run-of-the-mill salesman. What was happening? Well, among other things, his cancellation rate was just a hair under 50%!

As you can imagine, this was a problem worth taking a look at. And take a look we did! We monitored his sales calls, we sent people with him, and we interviewed his customers — those who had stuck and those who didn't. To put it mildly, we took him and his sales strategy apart, studied them, and put them back together again with some major changes.

First, we discovered he was playing fast and loose with the facts. Not bold-face lies, mind you. Just various "shades and hues" of the truth. And he would knowingly let customers

keep certain misconceptions without correcting them, his justification being that he didn't misinform them. He said they had
"come to the misunderstandings by themselves"!

O.K., let's say it out loud. There are only two ways to sell:
honestly or dishonestly. Not sort of honestly, almost honestly,
or only partially honestly. It's like you are either pregnant or
you aren't. Get it?

That simple understanding, coupled with the decision to
play honestly, will cut out the vast majority of cancellations in
any sales situation!

Any fool can see why bold-face lying will cost sales, so I
won't dwell on that. But the next subtle understanding is more
difficult to grasp.

All customers doubt the wisdom of their buying decisions. Many to a large degree, some to a very slight degree. But
they ALL carry the "doubt disease" within them. And all it
takes to set off the slumbering germ is one tiny little surprise. It
doesn't have to be big. It doesn't even have to be important. It
just has to be a surprise — something that conflicts with what
you told them. When that surprise or conflicting fact pops up,
you might as well have tossed a lit match into a room full of
gunpowder!

So first and foremost, sell **honestly,** plus some! And by
"plus some," I mean your customer should have a full, complete, and realistic understanding of what he just bought —
with **nothing** held back! Anything less gives him the excuse he
was looking for to pull the plug on your deal, as well he
should!

The next part of the cure was easier for our young friend
to deal with. Like many good salespeople, he was disorga-
nized. As a result, he didn't always follow through with the
small details he had promised while in the excitement of the
actual sales process. So we got him organized, in the habit of

251

writing things down, and in the habit of actually doing what he said he'd do before, during, *and* after the sale.

To help him understand this, I sent him to visit an old friend of mine. The man used to sell very expensive cars in Dallas, Texas. Very expensive.

The story he loves to tell on himself in order to help other salespeople is of the day he sold three Rolls Royce Corniches to one wealthy oil baron. One for the customer. One for the wife. One for the daughter. And the man paid with a personal check. A good one!

My friend said he'd have all three cars serviced and ready for pick-up by 3:00 PM that day. According to my friend, at 3:00 sharp the family was there with bells on their toes and stars in their eyes. They were as excited as young kids on their first big Christmas morning. Unfortunately, the cars weren't brought around until 3:20 PM — and, when they appeared, one had a light coat of dust on it, one needed vacuuming badly, and none of them had more than a quarter of a tank of gas!

My friend was horrified! The oil baron was furious!

What's the end of the story? Not a pleasant one, I'm afraid. The customer asked to use the telephone. First he called his bank and stopped payment on the check. Then he called one of his employees to come get him and his family. And off into the sunset he rode — probably to the country club, to tell all of his friends never to deal with my friend or that dealership again!

See? Sometimes it's the small things. How long would it have taken to vacuum one car? And to dust another? And how much money to gas all three? Virtually nothing! Yet the lack of those small touches cost my friend almost $500,000 in automobile sales (1980 dollars) and the substantial commission that should have gone with it!

And the final part of the cure for my young friend? The

post-sell! You simply *must* reassure your customers that they made the right decision. Spend time with them at the point of sale, then perhaps find an excuse to call them on some other matter, and finally, send them a thank-you letter/card/note — with a personal, handwritten message. We feel this is so important, Hampton Books offers a beautiful selection of thank-you cards designed exclusively for the professional salesperson.

Note: You are not only thanking them, you are reassuring them that they displayed excellent judgment when they decided to do business with you and your organization. Trust me, they were concerned about that. Don't let that concern grow, multiply, and destroy your sale!

Our young friend today? Well, he's got just a little grey at the temples now. He's still the top salesperson in that company — but now it's in both gross *and* net sales. And he has put together a sales career we'd all be proud to call our own. And so can you!

Only One Can Sell Price

Here's a quick one I heard one night in Seattle.

A sales trainer — one of the good ones — was holding an open sales seminar primarily for automobile salespeople. He was taking questions from the audience when a man asked what he should do since one dealership in town always had the lowest prices and he didn't work for them. He said he simply couldn't sell against that constant pricing problem. There must have been something to it, because others in the room quickly agreed it was a major problem.

Being a crafty old pro, the sales trainer looked sympathetic and encouraged others to sign on to the price problem. He quickly gained almost unanimous support for the proposition that it was virtually impossible to sell against this one low-cost dealership.

Then, with the crowd in a near frenzy of negative excitement, he put on his coat, put his manual in his briefcase, shut it, and started up the aisle — obviously a man on the way to the airport.

The crowd quickly quieted. Every eye was on him. He walked slowly, head down, a beaten man. Everyone could see he had finally faced the ultimate sales challenge and had no answer.

When he reached the door, he turned and said, "Ladies and gentlemen, I'm sorry. I've deceived you. I tried to get you to sell something other than the cheapest price. To sell service. To sell quality. To sell your own personal commitment to the customer. But it just dawned on me that you're right. And since by actual definition, only one company can offer the lowest price on any product or service, all others in that industry must be higher and, therefore, fail.

"Because of what I've learned here tonight, I now know that Seattle can only support one car dealership — the cheapest one. That the country can only support one automobile manufacturer — the cheapest one. And one computer company — the cheapest one. And one sales trainer — the cheapest one. And my friends, that *sure* isn't me!

"You see, although I wish I could do it, I can't be the cheapest sales trainer and still provide the quality of service I've decided to provide. It's economically impossible to provide the support services I provide and still be the cheapest. It has simply cost too much time and too much money to acquire the experience and knowledge I have to offer, to match the price of an inexperienced, uninformed, ignorant young sales trainer — the cheapest one on the circuit."

It was an amazing moment. Most were so taken aback by what he was saying, few noticed he was slowly moving back to the front of the room.

He continued. "You know, this is going to be devastating

when word gets out. No more Cadillacs. No more tailor-made suits. No more high-class restaurants. No more big homes. No more view lots. No more leather briefcases. No more quality appliances. No more quality anything. Just junk! Acres and acres of junk! And all of it offered by minimum-wage order-takers, because there'll be no need for salespeople of any kind. Just like it used to be in the old Communist countries. Yeah! That's it! We'll become a Communist country. That'll solve the price problem once and for all!"

You could've heard a pin drop. Suddenly, about a hundred salespeople *finally* understood the utter stupidity of allowing mere pricing to control their success or lack of it.

One more time: Never fall into the trap of selling price alone, or of even being drawn into that minefield. Your job — assuming you're selling quality products or services at even *close to* reasonable prices — is to build the value of your product, your service, your guarantee, your company, and *your own personal involvement* to the point that it exceeds the actual asking price. When it does, price becomes far less of an issue. In fact, it almost goes away!

Here's a good example of building value to the point of almost ignoring pricing. An automobile dealer in our area runs the usual spots you see on local television. Just like the ones in your area, they are poorly done, amateurishly produced, and mildly annoying. But each one ends with actual, local customers talking about their own personal experiences with the dealership. And the last person they always show is a lady who says, "I guess I'm one of Harold Ford's oldest customers. I've bought eight cars here in the last fourteen years. There is absolutely NO pressure. The prices are fair and the people are wonderful! The only thing I can't honestly vouch for is their Service Department . . . because I've never had to use it even once in all these years. I wouldn't even think of buying a car anywhere else!"

Note: Price wasn't, isn't, and won't be a factor with her when dealing with this dealership. They've sold her something else. No pressure, wonderful people, trouble-free cars . . . and fair prices! Not the cheapest in town. Just good, solid, dependable value!

Sales Infiltration

If I can explain the concept of Sales Infiltration, and if you can grasp the delicate subtlety of it, this chapter alone will make an enormous difference in your sales career. Let me go further than that. If you understand what I'm about to tell you, and if you can put it to work in your sales life, the system of Sales Infiltration can, by itself, take you to the very top of the sales profession.

Here's the danger of trying to explain it: It is going to sound so simple that the odds are you'll discount it, thinking "I already knew that." Trust me, you didn't!

Becoming an expert at Sales Infiltration, versus the vague and dim understanding most salespeople have of it, is like the difference between being a teenager who *thinks* he might want to be a doctor someday and the *world's finest* practicing brain surgeon.

First, what the word **"infiltrate"** means: "To cause (as a liquid) to permeate something by penetrating its pores. To pass through or into a substance by filtering or permeating. To pass troops singly or in small groups through gaps in the enemy line. To enter and become established in, gradually and unobtrusively, for subversive purposes."

Now go no further. Re-read the preceding paragraph *at least ten times!* If you want to be a real sales professional, memorize it! When understood, it is the beginning of one of the most important lessons you'll ever learn in selling, if not *the* most important lesson.

I know, directly or indirectly, just about everyone who is anyone in the English-speaking sales world. I'm talking about the true heavyweights of selling. And they all, to a man and to a woman, *without exception,* use this method of selling more than any other. In fact, they all use it all of the time, no matter what sales "technique" they may appear to be using. And no matter what you thought you saw them doing when you were trying to learn from them.

Just as infiltration is in actual warfare, Sales Infiltration is invisible. When done properly, you'll never see it! So you can't possibly learn it unless you read, devour, and absorb this chapter, or unless one of the sales heavyweights I referred to takes you under his or her wing and virtually adopts you. But since there are only about 1,000 of them on the entire planet at any given time, the odds of that happening are slim to none.

My friend, a major moment of truth has come for you. My ability to write and your ability to understand are what we have to work with. Don't let this opportunity pass you by, as only *you* will be hurt if you miss it.

If you are ready, the next few pages contain the **break-through** that will turn your entire sales career around.

First, understand why it is so difficult to learn from an actual practicing Sales Infiltrator. It's because they rarely, if ever, use a close. They *are* the close! They are a living, breathing close themselves. They have crossed over. They have transformed themselves. They have *become one* with their products, their services, their customers, their selling processes. The closes they tell you to use are, as best they can recall, what they used before their sales transformation. They don't need closing techniques now, as they are themselves the close! A living, breathing, walking, talking, sales-closing environment!

They'd like to help you. They really would. But they *can't* explain what they do, any more than you can explain the feelings or sensations of love, or anger, or remorse. You can *tell* me you are in love, but you can't make me *feel* what you feel. I have to discover that by myself, and then it will still be different than what you are experiencing!

So what do they do? They throw you a life preserver in the form of twenty or thirty pat closes and swear that's what they are doing! When, in fact, they wouldn't use those simplistic techniques on a bet. Not at gunpoint!

Don't misunderstand. They used to use those set closes before they became transformed. And they wouldn't have lasted in selling long enough to get to the very top if they hadn't! So they hope you will also survive long enough with the primitive tools of a sales amateur to evolve into a Sales Infiltrator — but percentage-wise, hardly anyone ever does. Maybe you will be the exception!

So why do all those guys with the fancy jewelry and neon-colored suits travel around the country teaching their sales-closing, buzzword-filled, hard-driving, almost absurd seminars? Well, many don't know any better. Some are actually trying to help you stay afloat long enough to find the truth for yourself. And all have come to discover that their audiences don't want abstract forms of difficult thought. They want it quick, easy, simple, and — oddly enough — funny!

So don't feel bad if you didn't get "it" at the last sales/ motivational rally you attended. It wasn't being offered. It is, however, offered in this chapter. And if you miss it this time, come back to this section again and again over the next few weeks, months, or years — whatever it takes! When the student is ready, the teacher will appear . . . and for a few of you, that teacher will begin to appear now.

Picture the typical selling situation. Whether you went to them or they came to you, it is "them" and "us." The battle lines are drawn. Your job is to sell, their job is to resist. No matter how good your product or service. No matter how reasonably priced. No matter how honorable your intentions. No matter how great their need. No matter how much you ache to prove you "aren't like all the others." The initial division is there. It always has been. It always will be. And you must learn to deal with what IS, not what you WISH was.

Faced with this situation hundreds of thousands of times a day all over the world, poor amateur salespeople, and most so-called closers, swing into action. They backslap and laugh, trying to buddy up to their customers. They want to be their pals. They don't know what else to do, so they pepper them with qualifiers, test them with trial closes, counter-punch with answers to objections, answer questions with questions, post-sell, resell, etc., etc.

Unfortunately, enough of them make enough money to make others believe that's the way to do it. And it is *a way to sell,* as far as it goes!

So what about those who make lots of money with these old-fashioned, clumsy techniques? Well, it proves what I told you earlier in this book: "Even a blind pig finds an acorn occasionally." And it certainly proves my long-held belief that "numbers" are a big part of selling. In other words, no matter how bad you are, if you call on enough people over enough time, you will make enough sales to eke out a living.

It follows that, if you get reasonably good and continue to make lots of sales presentations, you'll make an above-average income. And if you become a strong closer and make lots of sales presentations, you'll make a great deal of money, and will appear to the casual observer to be a top-notch sales-person.

The only difference between the first and last example is a little bit of skill — the type you can easily pick up from others. But you won't have begun to approach the level of a Sales Infiltration expert. You won't even be on the same playing field!

It's like what the golf pro said to a reporter one day. The reporter asked the pro what he thought about the way Jack Nicklaus played golf. The pro said, "Nicklaus doesn't play golf. The rest of us play golf. He plays something different."

Get it? Sales Infiltrators don't sell. Everyone else sells. They do something different!

Picture a room full of people dressed in expensive, tailor-made tuxedos. And there in the middle of them is one poor person in a cheap brown polyester leisure suit. That's what a salesperson or "closer" would look and feel like at a convention of Sales Infiltrators. He'd be outclassed. Embarrassed. Inadequate and humiliated. The difference is literally that great!

So you should be a sales "counselor," right? Wrong! That's just the next small step up from a run-of-the-mill sales-person. And, for some, it has been the end of their sales careers. Countless thousands of salespeople have "counseled" themselves out of the sales business. They became so warm and fuzzy they became totally ineffective. Loved, yes. Respected, maybe. But gone!

Understand, even a sales counselor is on "the other side." He or she may be warmer and more friendly, the dividing line may be softened, but it's still "them" and "us."

You must never lose sight of the only reason you are employed as a salesperson. *The only reason!* You are paid to obtain business your company wouldn't obtain if you weren't with them. Don't let all of today's touchy-feely success talk babble distract you. If you aren't getting your company sales they wouldn't get without you, you are just an extra expense . . . and they'd be better off without you!

Do I mean we are to return to the ancient days of "Dazzle them with our footwork and grab the money before they know what hit 'em?" Of course not! And I'm not saying that we shouldn't work to our customer's best advantage — always. (Remember the final lesson in *The Closers:* "Sum Tertius," or "I am third.") Nor am I suggesting *any* form of dishonesty at all. In fact, I believe in just about everything the best of the soft, warm-and-fuzzy sales trainers believe. And just about everything your minister or priest taught you. And your mother too! But, that said, there is NO excuse not to become the very best sales professional you can possibly be. That means being a Sales Infiltrator — to the extent your talent, ability, and willingness to work and learn will allow.

Again: Infiltrate means "To cause (as a liquid) to permeate something by penetrating its pores. To pass through or into a substance by filtering or permeating. To pass troops singly or in small groups through gaps in the enemy line. To enter and become established in, gradually and unobtrusively, for subversive purposes."

Now let's have no hang-ups about the strict dictionary definition. Your customers are not the enemy and you are not to be subversive in any negative sense. I just want you to understand what the word we are using so much ("infiltrate") actually means.

Now, let's reset the selling scene. The customer comes to you or you go to the customer — whichever. The true Sales Infiltrator, knowingly or unknowingly, goes to work on infiltrating the customer immediately, whether the customer is an individual, a family, a company, an organization, or any other identifiable entity. And I mean to the exclusion of virtually all other considerations. From this moment on, infiltrating the customer's side is the most important thing a Sales Infiltrator can do. And I don't mean just for the moment. I mean infiltration is an ongoing process that begins when you first see the customer, and continues until the very last day of your business relationship (when you die or retire from selling).

We aren't talking about you "selling" anymore. Nor "counseling." Those are both "them-and-us" situations. We aren't even talking about you becoming a trusted advisor. Advisors are still in the "them-and-us" game. We are going far beyond that — far beyond!

Sales Infiltrators actually become one with the customer. They "permeate the customer's pores. They pass through and into the customer. They enter through gaps in the customer's normal defenses. They enter and become established, gradually and unobtrusively, for *the good of the new entity.*"

Now pay attention. Here's the other side or part of this unbelievably powerful method of sharing your ideas, products, and services. If you have become one with the customer, they have, by definition, become one with you. There is no longer a buyer and a seller. There is a whole new unit and it is looking for solutions to its wants and/or needs.

In other words, you can't infiltrate them totally and completely without having them infiltrate you to the same degree. For example, if I pour a gallon of milk and a gallon of food coloring together, I no longer have the original two substances. I have an entirely new substance . . . and it is inseparable.

Why would you want to become one with the customer? Because it is best for the customer, best for you, best for all concerned!

You no longer have a salesperson trying to "sell" a defensive customer who is trying to "resist." You have a whole new unit made up of people who have a great deal to share with one another — for the *common* good. As the former customer/adversary, he or she can now open up and talk about the situation as they never would with an "outsider." And the former salesperson/adversary can now openly and honestly share the vital solutions he or she brought to the new entity.

You're on *their* team. They are on *your* team. But now it's the *same* team! NOT two friendly, cooperative teams. NOT two former enemy teams. The same team!

In this relationship, it is impossible to tell where one person begins and the other leaves off, because there is no seam. No trace of what once was!

You now have a full vote in the new entity — maybe the only vote in some situations! You are now part of the whole process. The selling. The buying. Everything!

It's like a partnership, but without the conflict, and it's a hundred times more effective and powerful!

An example: The casual observer might think the man who handles my insurance and estate planning is an insurance salesman and that I am the customer. But the casual observer would be dead wrong. His name is Mike Hunt and he is a Sales Infiltrator of the highest order. He doesn't sell me insurance. He doesn't recommend insurance. He buys insurance for me as *he sees fit* and sends me the paperwork to sign.

Mike long ago infiltrated my sales defenses. He is part of — for lack of a better way to explain it — Ben Gay, Inc. Like a Vice President, he tends to his duties regarding me and my family. The first and last "sales presentation" he gave to me was in 1967 . . . and that was to sell me on having him join my team. And me his. With that sale made, all other "selling" would be superfluous, exceeding what is sufficient or necessary.

And understand, I, too, am a Vice President of our endeavor. Not President over him. Not Assistant Vice President under him. Just a Vice President with *different* duties — like setting overall objectives and bringing in the money to make the other divisions possible. The Treasurer, if you will.

Get it? Mike has infiltrated me and my affairs. He can come up with an idea, implement it, pay for it, put it into effect, and never discuss the subject with me until after the fact. Nor do I call him to get permission to do my duties. We each have our separate responsibilities, but we're on the same team.

On the rare occasions when Mike feels it necessary to run something by me before taking action, the conversation has almost always ends with me saying, "Well, Mike, do whatever you think is right."

Who benefits from this type of relationship? Everyone! So much so that I seek Sales Infiltrators to infiltrate me. I don't want or need an enemy to call on me. I don't want to wonder what your motives are. I don't want to waste a single moment's sleep worrying about what you are up to. I want you, the salesperson of old, to forget about closing me, trapping me, or selling me. If you have good products and services, and if I'm a qualified prospect for them, I want to purchase them! I love to buy. And I want your help to do it! In fact, I want you on my team — as a full partner, specializing in your area of expertise. It makes my life easier!

After years of searching, I now have a top-notch "Vice President of Appliances" for my home. It's a little family business, and they even have the key to my house. They come and go unsupervised — just like any family member. If we need a new hot water heater, or garbage disposal, dishwasher, refrigerator, freezer, washer, or dryer, they install it and leave the bill on the kitchen counter. They check and service all of our appliances every six months — automatically. By infiltrating my sales defenses, they've made my life far easier and more enjoyable!

A great example of this particular partnership: We recently had problems with our old heat pump. The electric bill was up, but the equipment wasn't heating or cooling properly, so I called my Appliance Partners. A week or so later we came home and discovered we had a brand new space-age heating and cooling system that's the envy of all who enter our home. But on the kitchen counter was a bill from a company I'd never heard of. Turns out my Appliance Partners don't do heating and cooling systems. But did they tell me? No! They just handled everything for us for free, including a *very good* price — without breathing a word about it.

Now Mr. or Ms. Salesperson, do you honestly believe there is *any* tricky close, low-ball price, or other inducement you could use to get my appliance business away from these people? Trust me when I tell you that you couldn't get my business if you gave me *free* appliances! They have totally infiltrated my life. They are part of my family life. They have transformed themselves. They are one with me and my family. We aren't two warring camps. We are one functioning unit. They have, "as a liquid, permeated my pores. They have passed through me by permeating. They passed their family members singly and in groups through gaps in my line. They entered and became established in, gradually and unobtrusively, for *good* purposes."

Now here's a couple of twists for you to ponder:

The first example, Mike Hunt, has been a personal friend for many years. We've socialized. We've watched each other's family grow. We're pals. And Mike Hunt knew exactly what he was doing when he infiltrated my defenses. He is a *professional* Sales Infiltrator.

On the other hand, my friends who handle our appliances and our family's comfort and safety are not professional salespeople. I doubt they've ever heard the word "close." They don't even know there are sales seminars being held and they'd probably find them strange, indeed, as do I! I've never even laid eyes on my partners. Nor has any member of my family. They were referred to us by friends and have come to our home only during the day when we are all away.

Sales Infiltration is **subtle.** It isn't a contact sport! It can be done over the phone and even with notes on the kitchen counter. And when a Sales Infiltrator gets to a customer before you do, remove that prospect from your list of leads. You will *never* get that customer away — not until the first Sales Infiltrator retires or dies. It is the *ultimate degree,* the apex of selling.

So how do you become a Sales Infiltrator?

First, you must make the decision to do it. And you must believe, IN ADVANCE, that this is the way to run the rest of your sales career. You must commit yourself to the concept. It must become uppermost in your sales mind. You must visualize what your sales career would really be like if you had the keys to your customers' homes, bank accounts, hearts, minds, and souls. You must see yourself being held in high esteem and absolute trust by the people you wish to work with. Picture yourself as being worthy of having signatory control over the buying decisions of your customers. Imagine yourself as a person others admire and aspire to be!

If you can picture yourself becoming that type of person, and you are willing to take the action required, you are on your way to the very top of the sales world. You have taken the first steps.

Next, you must leave the world of schemes, inferior products, and rip-offs behind forever. You can't infiltrate the world of others and then betray them. For you, the days of the overpriced, low-quality swindles must be gone forever. You must cleanse yourself before you dare to ask for the trust and confidence of others.

You see, Sales Infiltration has a down side. If, after gaining the trust of someone to the degree we are discussing, you betray them in *any* manner, you will shatter the relationship forever. Callbacks, reselling, and post-selling won't save you. It's over. So, if you aren't prepared to walk this path for the rest of your days, don't start down it, whatever you do.

This is your first important test. If you aren't willing to forsake the world inhabited by low-level salespeople and con men, this entire section is a waste of your time. Go back to the hustle and grind of the workaday world of the amateur salesperson and forget you ever read this. Learn 25 more tricky closes, get yourself some more gold chains, and finish the job of wearing yourself out.

Search your soul. Are you *proud* of what you're selling? Would you want someone like you to be selling it to your mother right now? If not, resign! The world is full of companies with fantastic products and services that need a high-powered Sales Infiltrator to represent them. Go join one of them today!

If you're ready and willing to march on, you've got work to do.

This book has already covered much of the ground you need to learn and absorb, although you may not have realized it at the time. And there are many other books, audio and video cassettes, and seminars you need to expose yourself to. And don't forget the magazines and newspapers you'll need to broaden yourself. You must set out to become — if you aren't already — a person of class. A person others brag about knowing. A person capable of making others feel better about themselves just by being around you. An open, honest, and caring person. A person who can relate to others at a personal level almost instantly. A person who communicates clearly, effectively, and lovingly.

Aren't these all God-given talents some have and others don't? Yes, in the beginning that's true. There *are* people who are natural runners, swimmers, singers, dancers, and sales-people. Anyone who tells you otherwise is a liar or ignorant or both. It's not fair, but it's true nonetheless.

But, just like the natural singer practices to become the professional, you can work and improve your skills, talents, and abilities from their current level to a much higher level of accomplishment. Frankly, you may never reach the highest level of selling possible — you may not have the God-given talents of a Mike Hunt. But you can sure do a lot better than you are currently doing. You can sail to horizons of success and achievement you've only dreamed about. And with a great deal less wear and tear on you and your loved ones!

In order for you to get the concept of Sales Infiltration, I'm going to have to explain and re-explain it, and how to master it, from several different angles, so bear with me. I assure you it will be worth the time and effort if, end result, you get it.

I'm now going to tell you how I met my first Sales Infil-trator — at least the first one I recognized through hindsight. There were probably many others that I wasn't astute enough to catch!

Because I was a hard worker and reasonably well spoken for my age, I was promoted to the position of assistant buyer of the housewares department in the department store I told you about earlier, but at too young an age and with virtually no experience. That would have been O.K. with tight supervision, but the head buyer believed in letting you have your head, for better or worse! Further, he gave me complete buying control over the entire cookware section for the main downtown store and for each of several branch locations around the state. Believe me, I was in way over my head!

Enter Dick Dufano with Mirro Aluminum, Sales Infiltrator *extraordinaire!*

Dick was older than I, but of course, everyone was! He had an air of confidence and kindness about him. Without making me feel inferior, he instantly made it clear that *he* was trustworthy *(Note: Mirro Aluminum wasn't even an issue at that time, just Dick Dufano).* He gently let me know he was doing just fine already. I got the feeling that my next order, or lack of it, wasn't going to affect whether he and his family continued to eat or not. He was obviously successful and he was comfortable with that success.

We had a long, enjoyable conversation that first afternoon. We talked about many things. But, looking back, Mirro Aluminum cookware was the least of it. We talked about family — mine and his. We talked about golf. We talked about the challenge I was facing. We talked about how he could be of service and, since he knew many people in the industry, who else he could enlist to help me.

Then, at the time I expected him to whip out a catalog and begin hammering away at me about pots and pans, he ended the meeting and said he'd be in contact with some suggestions within a few days. Although we had known each other only a few hours, we parted friends.

A few days later, Dick called and invited me to join him for lunch. He said he had a few more questions to ask before he made any recommendations.

Lunch was in a very nice restaurant, several steps above the employee cafeteria I was used to, but not so nice as to make me feel uncomfortable.

During the lunch, our budding friendship was solidified and Dick offered to take me to a regional housewares convention that was being held the following week. What a relief! I was scared to death about attending it, and had already planned a good excuse to avoid going!

At the convention, my new friend took me to every single booth and introduced me to all of his competitors! He asked each of them to help me and work with me during my start-up phase, and showed me which of *their lines* I should carry, and the quantities!

A week or so later we played golf. I went home and met his family. Shortly thereafter I took him home to meet mine. We were buddies now. We had formed a **single unit.** He wasn't a salesman selling me and I wasn't a buyer surrounded by my defenses. We had common interests and common goals, which were for me to make that cookware department hum like it never had before — both in gross sales and in profits — and to make Dick Dufano the top salesman in the nation with Mirro Aluminum. That was our common goal. As you can see, it was a good situation for both of us IF we could make it work.

I won't leave you hanging. We did make it work! And we both got exactly what we wanted. Here's how we did it.

One day, thinking it was my idea, I asked Dick to meet with me. I told him that I had many other duties in the Housewares Department besides just cookware, and that I had no real desire to spend the next ten years learning as much as he already knew. But I DID want my first executive assignment to be a smash hit. So I proposed that he secretly take over complete control of the cookware section. I told him to write the orders, plan the promotions, and establish the basic model stock plan for all of the stores. He was to take inventory whenever he wanted, bring me the order that was to be placed, and I'd sign it without question.

271

The only thing I asked was that he take back his own mistakes. In other words, accept returns on any really over-stocked positions that might occur.

Now get this: I gave him this authority over all lines of cookware, not just Mirro's! He had control over Mirro, Regal-ware, Corningware, Presto, Farberware, etc., etc. ALL of them!

How did it work? Extremely well! With an expert in charge, the department broke all sales and profit records that year by substantial margins. He became Mirro's number one salesman and I was promoted to a head buyer's job. I was happy! Dick was happy! The store was happy! My "idea" was a smash success!

Now please fast-forward a couple of years. I'm in Chicago at the National Housewares Convention. I'm now a manufac-turer's representative calling on people, as Dick used to call on me. I wander into a sales training seminar and there stands a man explaining how to work with new buyers, assistant buyers, and old pros. The plan sounds amazingly familiar, so I sit down. Turns out the man is the national sales manager with Mirro Aluminum!

To make a long story somewhat shorter, he was explain-ing exactly how to "get close" to people. He didn't use the word "infiltrate," but it was the exact same process! And he said he'd only been able to completely teach his system to one other person. His name? *Dick Dufano!*

Then he gave an actual case study. From Dick's first meeting, to the day the new assistant buyer turned over the order book and told him to order whatever he wanted. Then he said he'd even give the name of the man in the best example he knew. I cringed! I held my breath! My ears were ringing! And then, out loud in front of God and everyone, he said the name of the assistant buyer. He said, "Many of you know him. His name is . . . Richard Oliver."

It wasn't me! There were others! Many others, it turned out! And we had ALL come to the exact same conclusion, independent of one another! We had ALL decided to give Dick our order books! We ALL thought it was our idea! We ALL prospered as a direct result! Every single one of us — including Dick Dufano!

Do you understand? Dick Dufano was a Sales Infiltrator. He never "sold" me a single pot, pan, or pressure cooker. He never had to! First he **infiltrated** me. Then we — together — ordered and sold more cookware than had ever been done before. We! A team! Not a closer, at war with a buyer. Dick and I became a single functioning unit. A unit with one purpose, not two. With one goal, not two. A unit based on "everyone wins"!

Want to take another look at Dick Dufano?

Dick dressed well. He walked confidently. He knew his products and his entire industry. **He put me first.** He was able to carry on a conversation on a wide range of subjects. He was kind. **He put me first.** He would meet me at any time of night or day. He would come early, stay late, and work weekends. **He put me first.** He knew when he didn't know and wasn't afraid to say so. He would never oversell me. **He put me first.** He scouted out other deals for me, even competing lines. He rejoiced when I succeeded. **He put me first.** He became a friend. He became a member of my family. **He put me first.** He stayed in contact. When we had a cookware sale, he was on the sales floor working with my salespeople. When we had warehouse sales, he stacked boxes and drove forklifts with the best of them. **He put me first. He put me first. He put me first.**

As a result, who did I put first? Dick Dufano!

Now just try to dream up a deal, promotion, or a close that would have gotten me to give you so much as a sample order during that period of time. Not for free could you have gotten your cookware into my store! Unless, of course, Dick Dufano had ordered it.

As a Sales Infiltrator, Dick Dufano had obtained the keys to my order book, warehouse, stockroom, and checkbook. And he did it with virtually *every account* he had in his territory!

More importantly, he NEVER violated that trust.

So the fact you sell widgets is certainly interesting, but not vital. There are lots of widgets out there. The fact you can explain your widgets is also interesting, but they could get almost anyone to do that. And the fact you are a hard closer probably amazes your friends and relatives at cocktail parties, but it won't cut it when you approach the top of this wonderful profession called selling.

Sales Infiltrators control their business. They have a lock on it. They've earned it.

I believe so much in Sales Infiltration that I now train the people I deal with to do it to me. I'm talking about when I'm the customer! I have Vice Presidents in charge of our home's cleaning and maintenance — inside and out. A Vice President in charge of all cars I buy. And a Vice President in charge of servicing them. A Vice President in charge of my suits. And one in charge of just about all other important areas of concern.

You'd want a steady, trusting relationship with your doctor, dentist, and lawyer. Why not all of the other professionals in your life, too? Doesn't that make sense? Wouldn't it make your life easier? Of course it would. And guess what. Your prospects and customers want the same thing from you . . . or from someone!

Here's what I do in the areas of my personal and business life that are important enough to be concerned about.

As soon as I isolate a salesperson who seems capable of understanding this rather simple concept, I sit down with him or her and in so many words say, "I've got a problem and I need your help. I'm tired of trying to outwit the amateur sales and service people in your industry. I want to give one person all of my widget business — all of it!

"Here's what I ask in return: that you treat me fairly, decently, and by the rules. That you give me good prices along with excellent products and services, all with fair and reasonable profit built in for you so you'll be happy to have my business and to service my account. I don't want you to lose money on me. Just give me the best deal you can, consistent with quality and service, and promise me no one else will be getting a better deal from you.

"When there is a situation where I'd be better off dealing with someone else, tell me. You and I will work out something that's fair for all and good for our *long-term* relationship.

"I want you to completely handle this aspect of my life and I merely ask that you never betray this trust. Are you willing to see if we can build a team on this simple foundation?"

You wouldn't believe the reaction! You wouldn't believe the service I get! Or the prices! Or the loyalty! And, because I try to return it tenfold, we all win!

Surely you are bright enough to establish that type of relationship with at least some of your customers! And when you do, you won't believe what it will do for your peace of mind, not to mention your net worth!

Now for those of you who sell items that are usually "one-call closes" like encyclopedias, vacuum cleaners, etc. Does the system of Sales Infiltration apply to you? Certainly. In fact, perhaps even more so!

Before we discuss the slight difference in approach so-called "one-call closers" need to use, let's get your thinking straight. Unless you are selling some "hit-and-run" scam, there is no such thing as a one-call close! You may only sell one encyclopedia set to this particular family on this particular evening, but a solid, long-term, well-cultivated relationship with them will give you an endless supply of prequalified, presold leads with which to work. And I mean endless! And I mean presold!

I have a friend in New England who was trained by J. Douglas Edwards. Doug caught him early, before he went on his first sales call about forty years ago. He sells cookware, china, silver, and crystal.

My friend was so stupid, he believed it when Doug told him that if he'd work his world-famous referral program properly, he'd only have to make one cold call in his life — just the very first one. Can you believe he'd be dumb enough to swallow that old line? Talk about stupidity!

Well, ignorance must be bliss, because my friend got five solid leads from his first sale (he's a natural Sales Infiltrator, as you may have guessed), and a total of thirty-six solid leads from those five new friends . . . and over a hundred from those new friends . . . and he's never looked back! And, just like Doug Edwards told him, except for his very first demonstration in 1957, he hasn't made a single "cold call" since. Sales Infiltrators lead much easier lives than do "normal" salespeople!

By the way, by staying in contact with almost every family he has ever sold with Christmas cards, birthday cards, yearly calls, etc., he continues to get fresh leads from his very first group of customers . . . almost forty years later! And he's delivered merchandise to their children and now to their grandchildren. You see, he is family! He is the "Vice President in charge of Cookware, China, Silver, and Crystal" for hundreds and hundreds of families throughout New England. You can do the same thing!

But how do you one-call closers get this firmly implanted on your very first call? What if your type of selling doesn't allow for several get-acquainted meetings? Then just do what my big Irish friend in New England does. Short-circuit the process. It gets the same basic result up front — then your get-acquainted meetings take place after the fact, through cards, letters, calls, etc. In fact, he often attends weddings, funerals, and all of the other events any other family member would attend.

Here's how he "shortcuts."

He tells them the *absolute truth* about the manner in which he prefers to work with his customers. **Before** he begins his demonstration, **before** he shows them a single item, he says, "As you've probably heard from [the family that referred him], I'm sort of an old-fashioned odd duck in the sales world. I only represent lines of merchandise I can be extremely proud of, and I prefer to work only with people who want quality in the products they purchase, and, more importantly, quality and service in the person who represents those products — with people I'd be proud to have as long-term friends. [The family that referred him] assured me you are my kind of people.

"You see, you can buy your cookware from lots of people, but only with the merchandise I'm going to show you this evening do you get *me* . . . and forgive me for bragging a little, but I'm an expert in this field.

"Now I can work with you two ways. If you want an old-fashioned, razzle-dazzle, high-pressure sales pitch, where we sell you a bunch of stuff you don't need and never see you again, I'll send over one of the company's young hotshots to do it to you. That's just not my style.

"But if you'll spend a little extra time with me, so we can discover what you *really* want and need now, and what you'll eventually like to acquire for your family over time, we can work together as friends and I can really be of service to you.

"Does that sound like a better arrangement for you? [pause] Would you feel comfortable working with me in that manner? [pause] Wonderful!

"Now before we get started, let me tell you what's in it for me. As friends, you should know that if the items you order tonight are all you *ever* order, you don't really need me . . . and, frankly speaking, there isn't going to be much in it for me either. So let me tell you that I'm looking at our new friendship over the *long-term*. I intend to earn your trust to the point that you think only of me and my products when you want or need the type of merchandise we represent. And, if I do my job properly, one day I'll have the pleasure of sitting in the homes of your children and, God willing, maybe even their children. Fair enough? [pause] Good!

"Are we ready to go to work? [pause] Great!

"O.K., let's see where we're starting from. Take me to your kitchen first!"

And off they go! Through the kitchen cabinets, the china hutch, the closets, the dining room — wherever he asks to look!

I just went back and timed the basic opening he uses and it took me about two minutes to say it comfortably. Add a couple of minutes for some reaction other than "yes" from the customers and you've got about a four-minute opening chat — max!

Do you think an extra four minutes of frank, straight-forward, totally honest conversation *before* you launch into your company's high-powered sales script might be worth-while? Remember, we are trying to launch a personal friend-ship and business relationship that might just last twenty, thirty, or forty years!

Before you go any further, go back and re-read what my friend says. Don't just look for the "friendship" lines. Look at the assumptive attitude! He clearly states they are *going to be ordering*. And he takes control of the situation because he is now a friend. An expert. A member of the family. The one who, in this area of their lives, will now *tell* them what to do —

to the extent of their financial abilities.

Once again, he is a **Sales Infiltrator!** He, as a liquid, permeates his customer's pores. He passes into them by filtering and permeating. He passes through gaps in their normal defensive line. He enters and becomes established in, gradually and unobtrusively, for mutually beneficial purposes.

And speaking of mutually beneficial purposes, understand that a Sales Infiltrator actually turns down business — lots of it! Why? Because sometimes the team, the family, the new unit simply shouldn't order, and the Sales Infiltrator is now an integral part of that new team. But here's the good news: Sales Infiltrators have enough extra business, because of the way they now operate, that turning down an order here or there is no longer the emotional and ethical temptation it once was. Not a bad way to live!

How do you do it? Start down the long path to becoming a person of class, quality, and absolute integrity. Associate yourself with products and services that are also of class, quality, and absolute integrity. And pretty soon you'll have a customer base of people who are also of class, quality, and absolute integrity. You see, like attracts like. It's a **Law of the Universe.** Just as sunrises are followed by sunsets and high tides by low tides. And just as spring is followed by summer, which is followed by fall and then followed by winter. That's just the way it works. Why? I really don't know, nor do I really care. I just try to work with what is.

And don't forget to constantly polish and hone your sales skills. Being a Sales Infiltrator does not excuse you from knowing all of the techniques of selling. In fact, it demands you know them. You are not to confuse being a Sales Infiltrator with becoming soft and ineffective. To the contrary! A Sales Infiltrator is devastatingly effective — that's the sheer power of the entire concept!

Now a few words about ethics:

Years ago I was in my sales training seminar with the legendary J. Douglas Edwards. He made a comment that I spent years coming to terms with. He said, "The only significant difference between a con man and a salesperson is belief in the products or services each is selling. The techniques are basically the same."

We could spend hours debating the finer points of that statement, and I still wrestle with it from time to time. But generalized and oversimplified as it is, there is a whole lot of truth to it, because the techniques for moving someone towards a decision know no morals. They are techniques, plain and simple. As with a gun, only you can determine whether those techniques are used for good or evil. And that puts a tremendous power, along with an equally tremendous responsibility, directly in your hands. But, as a Sales Infiltrator, you have an even greater opportunity and a corresponding problem before you. I alluded to it earlier, but let's revisit the subject.

If you are, for instance, a standard, run-of-the-mill, high-pressure, shiny-suited, gold-chained car salesman and you treat a customer less than fairly, you can actually get away with it to a certain extent. Here's why: Your industry is occupied by so many people like you, you get sort of a free ride. Your customers expect you to be sleazy. They consider it to be part of the car buying game. So they aren't especially offended by you. In fact, they might even buy from you in the future. At least you'll have the same shot at them as any other salesperson would have. Strange, but true!

If, however, you elect to become a Sales Infiltrator with all of the awesome power and responsibility that entails — if you are really able to become good enough to permeate a customer by permeating his or her pores; to pass through or into them by filtering and permeating; to pass through gaps in their defensive lines; to enter and become established in, gradually and unobtrusively, for good positive purposes — and then should you betray that trust in any manner, they will never have anything to do with you again . . . not ever. And they will tell many other people to also stay away from you! Your sales career will become a living nightmare.

Sales Infiltrator, average salesperson, or sales amateur? The choice is yours.

Until Next Time...

This is not the end. It is the beginning! You go to work on the personal improvement projects we've laid out and I'll start work on *The Closers - Part 3* this afternoon. We've both got our work cut out!

As I stated at the beginning of this book, the art of professional selling is not something that can be learned 1-2-3-4, like a waltz. Because no two sales situations will ever be the same, no one sales presentation is enough to make you a sales professional. Nor will any two sales presentations save you. Nor twenty-two. Nor fifty-two. Nor a hundred and two.

Sure, you'll see people knocking around the sales industry who manage to get by with high pressure and a set routine, but "get by" is the phrase to describe it. And if they are making $200,000 a year, it doesn't alter the fact that, with their obvious natural abilities and skills, they could be making $400,000 a year with no more effort, if they'd decide to get *serious* about the sales profession — and make no mistake, it is a profession.

I've mentioned J. Douglas Edwards several times. He made a good living for years traveling around the country talking about the Order Blank Close, the Alternate Choice Close, the Puppy Dog Close, the Ben Franklin Close, the Summary Question Close, the Similar Situation Close, the Call Back Close, the Lost Sale Close, the Secondary Question Close, the Trial Close, the Interim Close, the Final Close, the Negative Close, the See John Close, the Additional Close, the Visual Demonstration Close, etc., etc., etc.

It was terribly interesting listening to him. With his deep mesmerizing voice, he literally hypnotized thousands of people at a time. They wrote down every single word he uttered. They memorized the closes and then, like obedient parrots, they went forth and spewed their canned closes on the unsuspecting public. What happened? Well, 95% of them dropped out of selling, of course! And perhaps 5%, if that many, made it!

That rather startling statistic should drive you to ask the rather pregnant question, "What was different about the 5% who made it?"

Here it is: The 5% who made it were astute enough to realize that the specific pat closes were to be used as a base of understanding, a foundation on which to build. The closing techniques Doug taught were not the beginning and the end . . . just the beginning.

Now don't misunderstand, you should know all of those closes and a whole bunch more! That's how you learn what's going on during the sales process. The specific closes are also valid as an aid to your customers. They need and want to be channeled to a decision. That's why they are talking to you! But, that said, a true sales professional, a Master Closer, a Sales Infiltrator might live out his or her entire sales career and never deliver a single specific word-for-word close. Never!

Here's what the top professional heavyweights do: They use elements of some or all of those closes all of the time! They use the philosophy of the closes all of the time. For instance, moments ago I was writing the list of closes Doug Edwards taught. Frankly, I hadn't even thought of many of them in specific terms in many years. But I had to smile because, as I reviewed the list, I realized that I use elements of each of those closes almost every single time I'm in a selling situation!

Understand, it's been years since I've had to get out an order blank, start filling it out, and pray the customer didn't stop me. But I'm always talking as if the order blank was there and as if I fully intend to have it completed and approved.

And I don't really use the specific Alternative Choice Close anymore, but I always make sure my customers have a selection of choices before them at all times, and that all of those choices are positive for the selling situation, no matter what they select! In other words, we discuss whether they want delivery by ground or air, not whether they want delivery or not!

I listed sixteen of Doug's closes. I repeat, I can honestly tell you I haven't used a single one of them in years. I can also tell you that I used elements of all of them in a major sales presentation I made earlier this week. They are part of me now.

Here's an example that might help you. My youngest son is now taking karate lessons. He is busy learning a series of very specific moves. They're called codas, I believe. Some of them go on for several minutes, involving hundreds of precise moves, like a ballet. The moves are beautifully graceful and, of course, designed to be very damaging to the imaginary opponent.

Imaginary opponent! Got it? You see, my youngest son has a shock coming. I know because I watched our oldest son experience it just a few years ago. It was at his first karate tournament. He went out on the mat. The match began. He went into his coda routine and promptly found himself on his rear end. Seems the other kid was there to fight, not dance. They both knew their codas, but the other boy knew they were just a base of information from which to draw, not an end in themselves!

See? Just as it's not possible to lay out a karate match in advance, at least not blow by blow, kick by kick, it's not possible to lay out a sales situation in advance, at least not close by close. You should certainly know your sales "codas," but understand you may never use a single one exactly the way they were taught. You just have them there to draw from as needed.

While we're talking about karate, let me tell you about the man I selected to train both of our boys. He is an acknowledged karate master. A fifth-degree black belt in the Karate Kai school of discipline. And he makes an interesting study in being a master at something — anything, sales included.

Set the picture in your mind: The man is Asian-American. We live in what might be called a redneck area, out in the sticks with lots of loggers, cowboys, construction workers, and other types with pickup trucks, chain saws, and ugly dogs. The man is real small. The people that inhabit this area are larger than average. And my friend likes to square dance, which takes him into some cowboy, foot-stomping beer bars from time to time. Is that a formula for disaster if you ever heard one?

So I asked my friend if people were surprised when they picked a fight with him and were promptly rendered unconscious. His answer? "No one has ever picked a fight with me." In fact, no one has ever so much as suggested they would like to mess with him!

Seems that when you are near him, you just sense his confidence, power, and ability. He is a karate master. He has transformed himself. He has crossed over. He has become one with his skills, talents, and abilities. They aren't something he does, *outwardly*. They are something he is, *inwardly*.

A man who works at a nearby gas station told me about walking into a local bar one evening. A fight had broken out and just about everyone was involved. It was apparently a real brawl. But, as he looked across the dance floor, he spotted my karate master friend sitting at the bar, sipping a Coke, with a look of tranquility about him. Chairs were flying everywhere, but there he sat, untouched, with an invisible shield around him.

When next I saw him, I asked if the story was true. He confirmed it. Then I asked him when the invisible shield first went up and he said, "When I knew, that I knew, that I knew — then they *also* knew."

Here's a goal for you: Become such a professional, such a Master Closer, such a Sales Infiltrator, that you are one with yourself, your products, and your customers. Transform yourself! Cross over! *Become* the close! And do it to the point that you can honestly say and understand, "I know, that I know, that I know." And when you reach that level, they will also know, and they will treat you with the respect of a master salesperson.

And never forget, **"Sum Tertius." God first. The other person second. You are third.**

Ben Gay III

BEN GAY III

Born in Massachusetts and raised in Atlanta, Mr. Gay is considered one of the nation's top professional salesmen, sales trainers, and professional speakers. A charter member of the National Speakers Association, he has addressed nearly 300,000 people all over the free world. He's been a guest speaker at Dr. Schuller's famed Crystal Cathedral and has appeared on television and radio throughout North America.

In 1976 he pioneered the 800-number telecommunications industry, which today generates billions in yearly revenues, and is a mainstay of American marketing. Noted as being a "Super-Salesman," he's risen to the presidency of several corporations, including two of the nation's largest direct sales organizations.

Mr. Gay was dubbed "Attitude Coach" to the astronauts and ground crews of Apollo 15, 16 and 17. He also received national acclaim for his "People Builder's" success program, an exceptional educational experience which he created and ran for the inmates and staff of California's infamous San Quentin State Prison.

Ben Gay is the editor and/or author of many other books and cassette programs, including *The Closers, The Winner's Edge, Secrets of the Keymaster,* and *The Paragon Principle.* He is currently working on *The Closers - Part 3.* Mr. Gay and his family make their home in Northern California.

Additional Educational Titles from Hampton Books

The Closers

The Original Sales Closer's Bible!

Become a Sales Pro Overnight with the Famous Blue Book!

This is the famous *Blue Book* that has caused thousands of sales-people to double or even triple their earnings. The *Secret Book* that has boosted sales for hundreds of real estate developments, direct sales companies, insurance agencies, automotive dealer-ships, and every type of sales office across America. *The Closers* can do the same for you! Give the 300-page book a try. Better yet, try our "Super Deal," where you get $439.90 in FREE GIFTS!

– *Quantity Discounts Available* –

Item #2301 – *The Closers*: 300-page book - $24.95

Item #2401 – *The Closers*: 8½-hour, 15-cassette audio program - $99.95

Item #2501 – *The Closers Super Deal!* You receive the book, cassette program, *The Winner's Edge* book, *Closers Update Newsletter, The Paragon Principle* tape, and an additional 6 free business books of your choice. Total value is over $560.00! You invest just $119.90.

To order, call toll-free
800-248-3555
(ask for Operator #624)
Or use the handy order forms in the back of this book!

Welcome to Hampton Books

Your Full-Service
Mail Order Bookstore!

Any Title in the World!

Welcome to Hampton Books, your full-service book, audio, and video store! We represent virtually every publisher and author in the world, featuring 750,000 titles currently available. While most bookstores are limited by the number of titles on their shelves, Hampton Books is not. If we don't have a particular title in our distribution center, we will special order it at no extra charge and have it to you in a matter of days! Whether it's *Gone with the Wind* or the latest bestseller, our staff will get it for you!

Instant Shipping

We process and ship most orders within 24 hours of receipt! We ship most special orders within 7 working days. Our representatives will confirm your ship date when you place your order.

Our Guarantee

We guarantee satisfaction with this simple policy: If you're not happy with any purchase, for any reason, return it for a full no-questions-asked refund!

Call Us Toll-Free Today

We welcome you to the Hampton Books family and look forward to serving your needs. Remember, we're only a toll-free phone call away!

800-248-3555
(ask for Operator #624)

fax: (530) 677-1030
e-mail: closers@spider.lloyd.com

Box 67-8000 • Placerville, CA 95667-8000
Outside the U.S. call: (530) 622-7777